The Object Constraint Language
Language
Precise Modeling with UML

Jos B. Warmer
Anneke G. Kleppe

ADDISON-WESLEY

An Imprint of Addison Wesley Longman, Inc.

Reading, Massachusetts • Harlow, England • Menlo Park, California
Berkeley, California • Don Mills, Ontario • Sydney
Bonn • Amsterdam • Tokyo • Mexico City

Many of the designations used by manufacturers and sellers to distinguish their products are claimed as trademarks. Where those designations appear in this book and Addison-Wesley was aware of a trademark claim, the designations have been printed in initial caps or all caps.

The authors and publishers have taken care in the preparation of this book, but make no expressed or implied warranty of any kind and assume no responsibility for errors or omissions. No liability is assumed for incidental or consequential damages in connection with or arising out of the use of the information or programs contained herein.

The publisher offers discounts on this book when ordered in quantity for special sales. For more information, please contact:

Corporate, Government and Special Sales Group
Addison Wesley Longman, Inc.
One Jacob Way
Reading, Massachusetts 01867

Library of Congress Cataloging-in-Publication Data


```
Warmer, Jos B.
   The object constraint language : precise modeling with UML / Jos
 B. Warmer, Anneke G. Kleppe.
     p.      cm.
   Includes bibliographical references (p.    ) and index.
   ISBN 0-201-37940-6 (alk. paper)
   1. Object-oriented methods (Computer science) 2. UML (Computer
 science)    I. Kleppe, Anneke G.   II. Title.
 QA76.9.O35W37   1999
 005.1'17--dc21                                     98-29492
                                                        CIP
```

ISBN 0-201-37940-6
Text printed on recycled and acid-free paper.
1 2 3 4 5 6 7 8 9 10-MA-02010099
First printing, October 1998

The Addison-Wesley Object Technology Series

Grady Booch, Ivar Jacobson, and James Rumbaugh, Series Editors

For more information check out the series web site [http://www.awl.com /cseng/otseries/] as well as the pages on each book [http://www.awl.com/cseng/I-S-B-N/] (I-S-B-N represents the actual ISBN, including dashes).

David Bellin and Susan Suchman Simone,
The CRC Card Book
ISBN 0-201-89535-8

Grady Booch, *Object Solutions: Managing the Object-Oriented Project*
ISBN 0-8053-0594-7

Grady Booch, *Object-Oriented Analysis and Design with Applications, Second Edition*
ISBN 0-8053-5340-2

Grady Booch, James Rumbaugh, and Ivar Jacobson,
The Unified Modeling Language User Guide
ISBN 0-201-57168-4

Don Box, *Essential COM*
ISBN 0-201-63446-5

Don Box, Keith Brown, Tim Ewald, and Chris Sells, *Effective COM Programming: 50 Ways to Improve Your COM and MTS-based Applications*
ISBN 0-201-37968-6

Alistair Cockburn, *Surviving Object-Oriented Projects: A Manager's Guide*
ISBN 0-201-49834-0

Dave Collins, *Designing Object-Oriented User Interfaces*
ISBN 0-8053-5350-X

Bruce Powel Douglass, *Real-Time UML: Developing Efficient Objects for Embedded Systems*
ISBN 0-201-32579-9

Desmond F. D'Souza and Alan Cameron Wills,
Objects, Components, and Frameworks with UML: The Catalysis Approach
ISBN 0-201-31012-0

Martin Fowler, *Analysis Patterns: Reusable Object Models*
ISBN 0-201-89542-0

Martin Fowler with Kendall Scott, *UML Distilled: Applying the Standard Object Modeling Language*
ISBN 0-201-32563-2

Peter Heinckiens, *Building Scalable Database Applications: Object-Oriented Design, Architectures, and Implementations*
ISBN 0-201-31013-9

Ivar Jacobson, Grady Booch, and James Rumbaugh,
The Unified Software Development Process
ISBN 0-201-57169-2

Ivar Jacobson, Magnus Christerson, Patrik Jonsson, and Gunnar Overgaard, *Object-Oriented Software Engineering: A Use Case Driven Approach*
ISBN 0-201-54435-0

Ivar Jacobson, Maria Ericsson, and Agenta Jacobson,
The Object Advantage: Business Process Reengineering with Object Technology
ISBN 0-201-42289-1

Ivar Jacobson, Martin Griss, and Patrik Jonsson,
Software Reuse: Architecture, Process and Organization for Business Success
ISBN 0-201-92476-5

David Jordan, *C++ Object Databases: Programming with the ODMG Standard*
ISBN 0-201-63488-0

Philippe Kruchten, *The Rational Unified Process: An Introduction*
ISBN 0-201-60459-0

Wilf LaLonde, *Discovering Smalltalk*
ISBN 0-8053-2720-7

Lockheed Martin Advanced Concepts Center and Rational Software Corporation, *Succeeding with the Booch and OMT Methods: A Practical Approach*
ISBN 0-8053-2279-5

Thomas Mowbray and William Ruh, *Inside CORBA: Distributed Object Standards and Applications*
ISBN 0-201-89540-4

Ira Pohl, *Object-Oriented Programming Using C++, Second Edition*
ISBN 0-201-89550-1

Terry Quatrani, *Visual Modeling with Rational Rose and UML*
ISBN 0-201-61016-3

Walker Royce, *Software Project Management: A Unified Framework*
ISBN 0-201-30958-0

James Rumbaugh, Ivar Jacobson, and Grady Booch,
The Unified Modeling Language Reference Manual
ISBN 0-201-30998-X

Geri Schneider and Jason P. Winters, *Applying Use Cases: A Practical Guide*
ISBN 0-201-30981-5

Yen-Ping Shan and Ralph H. Earle, *Enterprise Computing with Objects: From Client/Server Environments to the Internet*
ISBN 0-201-32566-7

David N. Smith, *IBM Smalltalk: The Language*
ISBN 0-8053-0908-X

Daniel Tkach, Walter Fang, and Andrew So, *Visual Modeling Technique: Object Technology Using Visual Programming*
ISBN 0-8053-2574-3

Daniel Tkach and Richard Puttick, *Object Technology in Application Development, Second Edition*
ISBN 0-201-49833-2

Jos Warmer and Anneke Kleppe, *The Object Constraint Language: Precise Modeling with UML*
ISBN 0-201-37940-6

Contents

Chapter 4
Modeling with Constraints

Chapter 5
Extending OCL

Appendix A
OCL Basic Types
and Collection Types

Appendix B
Formal Grammar

Bibliography

Index

List of Figures

List of Tables

Foreword

For many years there has been a branch of computer science concerned with using formal logical languages to give precise and unambiguous descriptions of things. As an academic in the 1970s and 1980s I was very interested in such languages, for example Z and Larch. Unravelling the meaning of a statement in one of these languages is sometimes like a complex jigsaw puzzle, but once the unravelling is done the meaning is always crystal-clear and unambiguous. As I moved into the world of object-oriented methods I found a different way of specifying, using diagrams. With diagrams, the meaning is quite obvious, because once you understand how the basic elements of the diagram fit together, the meaning literally stares you in the face.

But there are many subtleties and nuances of meaning that diagrams cannot convey by themselves: uniqueness, derivation, limits, constraints, etc. So it occurred to me that from a modelling perspective a carefully designed combination of diagrammatic and formal languages would offer the best of both worlds. Armed with this realisation I worked during the early 1990s with John Daniels to create Syntropy, an object-oriented modelling language which combined the diagrammatic simplicity and clarity of OMT with the formality of a subset of Z.

Object Constraint Language (OCL) was first developed in 1995 during a business modelling project within IBM in which both Jos Warmer and I were involved, working in IBM's Object Technology Practice. This project was heavily influenced by Syntropy ideas. But unlike in Syntropy there is no use in OCL of unfamiliar mathematical symbols. OCL was very carefully designed to be both formal and simple: its syntax is very straightforward and can be picked up in a few minutes by anybody reasonably familiar with modelling or programming concepts.

During 1996 Jos and I became involved in the Object Management Group's efforts to standardize on a language for object-oriented analysis and design. I led IBM's contribution to this process, and together with ObjecTime Limited we wrote a proposal which emphasised simplicity and precision. Our goal all along was to collaborate with the other submitters to produce an overall standard containing the right elements in the right balance. OCL was a fundamental aspect of this proposal.

The leading proposal was UML (Unified Modeling Language) from Rational Software Corporation and its partners. UML, which combined ideas from its three authors Grady Booch, Ivar Jacobson, and James Rumbaugh, focused primarily on the diagrammatic elements and gave meaning to those elements through English text. As the submissions were combined, OCL was used to give added precision to the definition of UML; in addition OCL became part of the standard and thus available to modellers to express those additional nuances of meaning which just the diagrams cannot represent. This is a very important addition to the standard language of object-oriented modelling.

Jos Warmer and Anneke Kleppe's book is a crucial addition to the object-oriented modeling literature. I've greatly enjoyed working with Jos on the development of OCL over the past few years, and he and Anneke have done a first-class job in this book of explaining OCL and making it accessible to modellers. They have focused on the important aspects and illustrated the concepts with plenty of simple examples. Even for those with no experience of formal methods this book is an excellent place to learn how to add precision and detail to your models.

Steve Cook

Steve Cook is the lead architect of IBM's European Object Technology Practice. He has been a pioneer of object-oriented methods and technologies for 20 years. He founded the OOPS specialist group of the British Computer Society in 1985, and the Object Technology series of conferences held in the UK annually since 1993. He was Managing Director of Object Designers Ltd from 1989 until 1994, when he joined IBM. In 1998 he was awarded an Honorary Doctor of Science degree by De Montford University.

Preface

In November 1997, the Object Management Group (OMG) set a standard for object-oriented analysis and design facilities. The standard, known as the Unified Modeling Language (UML), includes model diagrams, their semantics, and an interchange format between CASE tools. Within UML, the Object Constraint Language (OCL) is the standard for specifying invariants, preconditions, postconditions, and other kinds of constraints.

The only way we can gain anything from a standard is if everyone uses it. Therefore, any standard should be easy to use, easy to learn, and easy to understand. These objectives were our guidelines during the development of OCL.

OCL can be called a "formal" language, but unlike other currently available formal languages such as Objective-Z or VDM++, OCL is not designed for people who have a strong mathematical background. The users of OCL are the same people as the users of UML: software developers with an interest in object technology. OCL is designed for usability, although it is underpinned by mathematical set theory and logic.

Our objective in writing this book is to offer to practitioners of object technology a convenient way to become acquainted with and make use of this part of the UML standard. By writing this book we intend to make OCL available to everyone who can benefit from it. Using, learning, and communicating with OCL should be easy, and this book is an effort to make it easy.

With this book we emphasize the importance of constraints in object-oriented analysis and design and the importance of a formal, separate language for constraint notation. Please take OCL and use it well, so that the whole object-oriented community will gain from your efforts.

ACKNOWLEDGMENTS

Although on the cover of any book only the names of the authors appear, a book is always the result of the blood, sweat, and tears of many people. For their efforts in reviewing this book we would like to thank Balbir Barn, Steve Cook, Wilfried van Hulzen, John Hogg, Jim Odell, and Cor Warmer. Special thanks go to Heidi Kuehn, who did a great job polishing our English.

Acknowledgments for their contributions to OCL must undoubtedly go to the following:

- The IBM team that developed the first version of OCL: Mark Skipper, Anna Karatza, Aldo Eisma, Steve Cook, and Jos Warmer.
- The joint submission team from IBM and ObjecTime. The ObjecTime team was composed of John Hogg, Bran Selic, and Garth Gullekson, and the IBM team consisted of Steve Cook, Dipayan Gangopadhyay, Mike Meier, Subrata Mitra, and Jos Warmer. On an individual basis, Marc Saaltink, Alan Wills, and Anneke Kleppe also contributed.
- The UML 1.1 team, especially the semi-formal subgroup of the UML core team: Guus Ramackers, Gunnar Overgaard, and Jos Warmer.
- Several people who influenced OCL during this period, most notably Desmond D'Souza, Alan Wills, Steve Cook, John Hogg, and James Rumbaugh.
- The many persons who gave their feedback on the earlier versions of OCL.

We would also like to thank all our teachers, colleagues, clients, and friends who in the past 15 years made us aware of the need for a practical form of formalism in software development. Coming from a theoretical background (mathematics and theoretical computer science), we have always found sound formalisms appealing, but very early in our careers we decided that writing a two-page "proof" for five lines of code is not the right way to improve our software. We have been searching ever since for a way to combine our love for sound and complete formalisms with our sense of practicality. We hope and expect that OCL will turn out to be just that: a practical formalism.

Anneke Kleppe and Jos Warmer

October 1998, Soest, Netherlands

Introduction

The Object Constraint Language (OCL) is an expression language that enables one to describe constraints on object-oriented models and other object modeling artifacts.

A *constraint* is a restriction on one or more values of (part of) an object-oriented model or system. OCL is part of the Unified Modeling Language (UML), the Object Management Group (OMG) standard for object-oriented analysis and design. OCL is formally defined in *Object Constraint Language Specification* [OCL97].

Several books on UML have been published. Most of them focus on the diagramming techniques and pay less attention to constraints. The books based on UML version 1.0 do not refer to OCL at all, because OCL was added in version 1.1.

Although several object-oriented modeling methods (Syntropy [Cook94], Catalysis [D'Souza98], and BON [Walden95]) use constraint languages, constraints are relatively new to object modeling. Therefore, we think it is useful to have a book dedicated to this part of UML.

WHO SHOULD READ THIS BOOK

The book is meant to be a textbook and reference manual for practitioners of object technology who find a need for more precise modeling. These people will want to use OCL in their analysis and design tasks, most probably within the context of UML but potentially with other object modeling languages.

This book assumes that you have general knowledge of object-oriented modeling, preferably UML. If you lack this knowledge, there are many books on UML that you can choose from.

HOW THIS BOOK SHOULD BE USED

If you are unsure whether to use constraints, read Chapter 1, Why Write Constraints?

If you are in a hurry, you might want to read only Appendix A, OCL Basic Types and Collection Types, and Appendix B, Formal Grammar, and then trust your intuition.

If you have a little more time, you can read Chapter 2, OCL Basics, and then start using OCL. When you are sure that you have made serious mistakes, you can read Chapter 3, The Complete Overview of OCL Constructs, and Chapter 4, Modeling with Constraints. They contain information about styles, constraint contexts, and so on.

If you want to study OCL in more depth but you don't have enough time to read the complete book, you can read Chapter 2, OCL Basics, Chapter 3, The Complete Overview of OCL Constructs, and Chapter 4, Modeling with Constraints.

Chapter 5, Extending OCL, is meant for advanced users of OCL. If you see more opportunities to use OCL but lack the language constructs to do so, you should read this chapter. If it does not answer your questions, it is time to contact one of the authors.

TYPEFACE CONVENTIONS

This book uses the following typeface conventions:

- All OCL expressions are printed in a monospaced font.
- The context to which an OCL expression applies is printed in a monospaced font and underlined:

    ```
    OCLcontext
    OCLexpression
    ```

- At the first introduction or definition of a term, the term is shown in italics.
- All references to classes, attributes, and other elements of a UML model are shown in italics.

INFORMATION ON RELATED SUBJECTS

The text of the UML standard, including OCL, is freely available on the OMG Web site (http://www.omg.org) and the Rational Corporation Web site (http://www.rational.com). More information on UML can be found in the following:

- *Unified Modeling Language User Guide,* by Grady Booch, James Rumbaugh, and Ivar Jacobson
- *Unified Modeling Language Reference Manual,* by James Rumbaugh, Grady Booch, and Ivar Jacobson

- *The Objectory Software Development Process*, by Ivar Jacobson, Grady Booch, and James Rumbaugh

OCL is a new language that is still growing and maturing. Recent information on OCL, as well as a free parser, can be found on IBM's Web site:

- http://www.software.ibm.com/ad/ocl

The Klasse Objecten Web site also contains OCL information:

- http://www.klasse.nl/Engels/ocl.htm

Chapter 1

Why Write Constraints?

This chapter defines the concept of constraints. It discusses the definitions that have been in use so far and explains why constraints are useful when describing and developing object-oriented business models and applications.

1.1 DEFINITION OF CONSTRAINT

In the introduction of this book, we defined a constraint as follows:

> *A constraint is a restriction on one or more values of (part of) an object-oriented model or system.*

But what exactly do we mean by that? To answer this question, we first look at the use of constraints in various object-oriented techniques. Section 2.5 explains the design choices made for OCL and discusses the reasons for these choices.

1.1.1 Use of Constraints in Other Techniques

What we call a constraint has been known in object technology for some time under various names. Bertrand Meyer was one of the first people to recognize its use. His term for a constraint is *assertion*, which he defines as "an expression of the element's purpose" [Meyer88]. Assertions as defined by Meyer come in three flavors—preconditions, postconditions, and invariants—all of them defined locally to the class. They have been implemented in the Eiffel programming language, where they form the basis for the design by contract principle. This principle is explained in the following section.

Ian Graham uses both the concept of *assertion* and the concept of *rule*. He defines assertion as "invariance, precondition and postcondition facets: conditions that must hold when the method is running, fires and terminates respectively" [Graham95]. His rule concept, which is derived from knowledge-based systems, expresses the semantics of how one object is influenced by another.

The term *constraint* is defined by James Rumbaugh et al. as a "functional relationship between entities of an object model" [Rumbaugh91]. In their analysis and design method, OMT, constraints restrict the values that entities can assume.

Grady Booch also uses the term *constraint,* which he defines as "the expression of some semantic condition that must be preserved" [Booch94]. He stresses the fact that a constraint can be preserved only while the system is in a steady state. There may be temporary circumstances in which the constraints on the system will not be valid.

There are many different interpretations of the concept of constraint, each of which has a different focus. OCL tries to express the common factor, thereby setting a standard that is understandable and easy to use and allows the modeler to specify what is necessary.

1.2   DESIGN BY CONTRACT

An effective way to specify operations and methods is the use of pre- and postconditions. Within UML, we can use OCL expressions to specify the pre- and postconditions of operations and methods on all classes, types, and interfaces. The principle behind the use of pre- and postconditions is often referred to as the *design by contract* principle. Design by contract can be used within the context of any object-oriented development method. It is the basis of a genuine *software engineering* approach. The following paragraphs describe the principle and its advantages.

1.2.1   Definition of Contract

The definition of *contract* in the design by contract principle is derived from the legal notion of a contract: a univocal lawful agreement between two parties in which both parties accept obligations and on which both parties can found their rights. In object-oriented terms, a contract is a means to establish the responsibilities of an object clearly and unambiguously. An object is responsible for executing services (the obligations) if and only if certain stipulations (the rights) are fulfilled. A contract is an exact specification of the interface of an object. All objects that are willing to use the services offered are called *clients* or *consumers.* The object that is offering the services is called the *supplier.*

Although the notion of contract is derived from law practice, it is not completely analogous when employed in object technology. A contract is offered by an object independently of the presence of any client. But when a client uses the services offered in the contract, the client is bound to the conditions in the contract.

1.2.2 Contents of a Contract

A contract describes the services that are provided by an object. For each service, it specifically describes two things:

- The conditions under which the service will be provided
- A specification of the result of the service that is provided, given that the conditions are fulfilled

An example of a contract can be found at most mailing boxes in the Netherlands:

> *A letter posted before 18:00 will be delivered on the next working day to any address in the Netherlands.*

A contract for an express service is another example:

> *For the price of four guilders, a letter with a maximum weight of 80 grams will be delivered anywhere in the Netherlands within 4 hours after pickup.*

A contract can become much more complicated, for example, when it concerns the purchase of a house. The important thing is that the rights and obligations in a contract are unambiguous. In software terms we call this a *formal specification*.

1.2.3 Advantages of Contracts

Both parties benefit from a clear contract.

- The supplier knows the exact conditions under which its services can be used. If the client does not live up to its obligations, the supplier is not responsible for the consequences. This means that the supplier can assume that the conditions are *always* met.
- The client knows the exact conditions under which it may or may not use the offered services. If the client takes care that the conditions are met, the correct execution of the service is guaranteed.

If either party fails to meet the conditions in the contract, the contract is broken. When this happens, it is clear which party broke the contract: either the client did not meet the specified conditions, or the supplier did not execute the service correctly.

Table 1-1 shows the rights and obligations of both parties in the express delivery service example. Note that the rights of one party can be directly mapped to the obligations of the other party.

Table 1-1 *Rights and obligations in a contract.*

Party	Obligations	Rights
Customer	Paying five guilders	Letter delivered within 4 hours
	Supply letter with weight less than 80 grams	
	Specify delivery address within Netherlands	
Express service company	Deliver letter within 4 hours	Delivery addresses are within the Netherlands
		Receive five guilders
		All letters weigh less than 80 grams

1.2.4 Preconditions and Postconditions

The interface that is offered by an object consists of a number of operations that can be performed by the object. For each operation, the rights of the object that offers the contract are specified by preconditions. A *precondition* must be true at the moment that the operation is going to be executed. The obligations are specified by postconditions. A *postcondition* must be true at the moment that the operation has just ended its execution.

Failure of a pre- or postcondition—that is, the condition is not true when it should be—means that the contract is broken. In Eiffel, the only language that implements the design by contract principle, an exception is raised when a pre- or postcondition fails. In this way the exception mechanism is an integral part of the design by contract principle.

1.2.5 Invariants

In addition to the pre- and postconditions, Bertrand Meyer defines a third kind of constraint: the invariant. Invariants are always coupled to classes, types, or interfaces.

An *invariant* is a constraint that states a condition that must always be met by all instances of the class, type, or interface. An invariant is described using an expression that evaluates to true if the invariant is met. Invariants must be true all the time. Pre- and postconditions need be true only at a certain point in time: before and after execution of an operation, respectively.

In UML, these three uses of constraints are predefined as three standard stereotypes of UML constraints: *<<invariant>>*, *<<precondition>>*, and *<<postcondition>>*.

1.3 ADVANTAGES OF CONSTRAINTS

Constraints convey a number of benefits.

1.3.1 Better Documentation

Constraints add to the visual models information about the model elements and their relationships. Therefore they are an excellent form of documentation. Constraints must be kept close to the model. Versioning of the constraints should be in accordance with the versioning of the model(s) to which they apply.

A visual model itself may also contain some constraints, although we might not think of them as such. For example, the multiplicity at an association end in a class model is a constraint on the number of object instances that can be linked. Using OCL, you can specify many additional kinds of constraints.

1.3.2 Improved Precision

Constraints cannot be interpreted differently by different people. They are unambiguous and make more precise the model or system to which they apply.

When you use OCL to express constraints, you can use an OCL parser to ensure that the constraints are well formed and meaningful within the model. Such checking helps you to create a correct and precise model or system. A prototype of an OCL parser written in the Java language is freely available on IBM's Web site: http://www.software.ibm.com/ad/ocl.

1.3.3 Communication without Misunderstanding

Models are used to communicate among users, modelers, programmers, and other people. Flawed communication is responsible for the failure of many software projects. Most models are accompanied by a natural language explanation to help the receiving party understand the model. But readers often must rely on their own interpretation. Using OCL constraints, the modeler can unambiguously communicate his or her intent to all other parties. Misunderstandings can be caught earlier in the software development process, thereby saving both frustration and money.

1.4 DECLARATIVE OR OPERATIONAL CONSTRAINTS

All interpretations of constraints seem to agree that they are necessary for expressing restrictions on the objects in the system or model that must be true for the model or system to be correct or consistent. Another important point learned from experience is that constraints add information that otherwise cannot be expressed in the models.

What differs in the interpretation of constraints is how one should react when a constraint is broken, in other words what action has to be taken when the restrictions laid on the objects are no longer met.

Some people argue that a constraint is purely a declaration of what must be true, not of what should be done. We call such constraints *declarative constraints*. In UML, constraints are expressed in a declarative manner, although its writers realized that in a programming language constraints should be expressed in operations, thereby making the constraint concept a pure modeling technique.

Others argue that breaking a constraint should throw some kind of exception, or at least that such behavior should be an option. In Eiffel, assertions are used as a debugging tool and as an exception facility; this means that when the assertion (or in our terms the constraint) is broken, an exception is thrown.

Still others argue that the breaking of a constraint is a trigger for an operation to be executed. We call these kinds of constraints *operational constraints*. In Soma, the analysis and design method defined by Ian Graham, rules can be triggers to actions that the system must undertake.

1.4.1 Advantages of a Declarative Language

In a declarative language, constraints have no side effects; that is, the state of a system does not change because of the evaluation of an expression. There are three advantages to this interpretation.

First, the modeler need not decide how the breaking of a constraint should be handled. True, this question has to be addressed at some point, but you can divide and conquer the problem. First, the modeler decides which constraints must be valid. Later, the modeler or someone else decides how to resolve problems that occur when the constraints are broken. This approach results in a clear separation between specification and implementation.

The second advantage is that constraints should be stable within their domains; that is, they should not change much over time. The actions that need to be undertaken when the constraints are not met change more often or can be different from one application to another within the same domain.

The third advantage is that when constraints are checked with the aim to perform an action on them, the check must be regarded as one atomic action. If the values on which a constraint depends can change during the evaluation of the constraint, the outcome of that check is not reliable.

1.5 NOTATION: NATURAL LANGUAGE OR MATHEMATICAL EXPRESSIONS

Once we agree that the use of constraints is essential to express certain information about an object-oriented model or application, we are ready to discuss the constraint notation.

The first option is to use natural language. People usually express themselves well in their own language, but is a constraint in natural language clear and precise enough for the purpose of modeling business and software systems? Research on automatic translation shows that conversations in natural language rely heavily on the understanding and implicit assumptions of those involved. If, for example, two people know that the subject of their conversation is a specific woman named Susan, they might have a shared understanding of the phrase "She just can't live without him." If the two people have just met at a party, one of them might think that the phrase is the title of the song that is playing.

When using constraints to model or describe an application, we want to express information that cannot otherwise be expressed. If the notation we choose means that this information can be understood only by people who already have a great deal of understanding of the domain, then we have missed the mark. The model must also be understood by people who are new to the domain and lack the necessary domain knowledge.

Another point about natural language is that people tend to express themselves imprecisely or even ambiguously. One often hears phrases such as "Did you see that? Far out." The speaker doesn't state what object *that* refers to. It could be a flying saucer, a bird, the hairdo of a strange person, or any other object. As has been well put by Steve Cook and John Daniels [Cook94], there is a difference between precision and detail. In object-oriented modeling, we often leave out the details, but at the same time we need the precision.

Sometimes people refer to what they call "precise English" as being the right way to write unambiguous constraints. Practice has taught us that even precise English is ambiguous. See, for example, the paper "On formalism in specifications" [Meyer85], in which a very carefully written specification is dissected and shown to be ambiguous. It is also interesting to note that the initial version of UML (1.0) submitted to the OMG for standardization was written using precise English. This initial version received much feedback concerning its many ambiguities and inconsistencies. As a result, UML adopted OCL as its constraint language, and the final UML 1.1 standard is described using OCL. We conclude that natural language is not the right choice for a constraint notation.

The second option for a constraint notation is some kind of mathematical notation. All experience with formal or mathematical notations leads to the same conclusion: The people who can use the notation can express things precisely and unambiguously, but very few people can really use such a notation. Although it seems a good candidate for a precise, unambiguous notation, a mathematical notation cannot be used as a standard constraint language. The aim of a standard is that it be widely used and not that it be exact but rarely used.

We need the rigor and precision of mathematics, but the ease of use of natural language. These are conflicting requirements, so we need to find the right balance.

1.6 SUMMARY: REQUIREMENTS FOR OCL

Having considered the discussion in the earlier sections of this chapter, we can now explain our definition of constraint.

> *A constraint is a restriction on one or more values of (part of) an object-oriented model or system.*

In practice, there are many restrictions on the objects and classes in an object-oriented model that cannot (without great difficulty) be specified in a visual representation. We call these restrictions constraints. A constraint is an expression that gives extra information on (part of) a visual object-oriented model or artifact.

Constraints always apply to the elements of an object-oriented model or system, and they always restrict values of these elements. Constraints must be true at a given moment in time for the model or artifact to be valid.

The earlier sections of this chapter have also led us to a number of requirements for OCL.

1. OCL must be a language that can express extra (necessary) information on the models and other artifacts used in object-oriented development.
2. OCL must be a precise, unambiguous language that can easily be read and written by all practitioners of object technology and by their customers. This means that the language must be understood by people who are not mathematicians or computer scientists.
3. OCL must be a declarative language. Its expressions can have no side effects; that is, the state of a system must not change because of an OCL expression.[1] If a constraint does not hold at a certain moment, then the model or system is not valid and action should be undertaken to restore it to a proper state. Note that the actions to be taken are not specified in OCL.
4. OCL must be a typed language. OCL expressions will be used mainly for modeling and specification purposes. Because most models are not (yet) executable, most OCL expressions will not be executed. However, it must be possible to check an OCL expression without an executable version of the model. As a

---

[1] We foresee the desire for an extension to OCL that couples denotational constraints and operational semantics. Chapter 5 gives some information on this subject.

typed language, OCL expressions can be checked during modeling, before execution.

This chapter summarizes the foundations on which OCL was built. The following chapters discuss how OCL meets these requirements.

Chapter 2

OCL Basics

The sample system in this chapter provides a short and informal introduction to OCL. A more complete and rigorous description of OCL can be found in Chapter 3. After reading this chapter you will be able to add simple OCL constraints to your own UML models.

Section 2.1 introduces the example class model and description that is used in this book. By their nature, constraints exist within the context of an object-oriented model or application. They are not stand-alone; they cannot exist without the structural model of the objects whose values they restrict. All examples of OCL expressions in this chapter and Chapter 3 are therefore linked to one of the class diagrams described in the example.

2.1 THE "ROYAL AND LOYAL" SYSTEM EXAMPLE

As an example, we have modeled a computer system for a fictional company called Royal and Loyal (R&L). R&L handles loyalty programs for companies that offer their (good) customers various kinds of bonuses. Often, the extras take the form of bonus points or air miles, but other bonuses are possible as well: reduced rates, a larger car for the same price as a standard rental car, extra or better service on an airline, and so on. Anything a company is willing to offer can be a service rendered in a loyalty program. Figure 2-1 shows the UML class model R&L uses for most of its clients.

The central class in the model is *LoyaltyProgram*. A system that administers a single loyalty program will contain only one object of this class. A company that offers its customers a membership in a loyalty program is called a *ProgramPartner*. More than one company can enter into the same program. In that case, customers who enter the loyalty program can profit from services rendered by any of the participating companies.

Every customer of every program partner can enter the loyalty program by filling in a form and obtaining a membership card. The objects of class *Customer* rep-

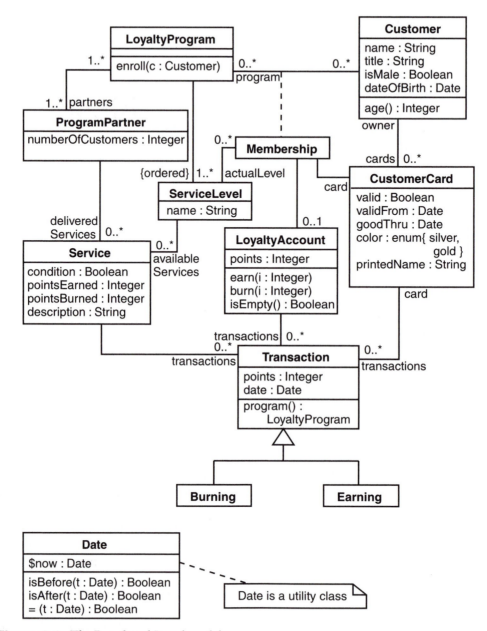

Figure 2-1 *The Royal and Loyal model.*

resent the people who have entered the program. The membership card, represented by the class *CustomerCard*, is issued to one person. Card use is not checked, so the card could be used as a family or business card. Most loyalty programs allow customers to save bonus points. Each individual program partner decides when and how many bonus points are allotted for a certain purchase. Saved bonus points can be used to "buy" specific services from one of the program partners. To account for the bonus points that are saved by a customer, every membership can be associated with a *LoyaltyAccount*.

Various transactions on this account are possible. For example, the loyalty program "Silver and Gold" has four program partners: a supermarket, a line of gas stations, a car rental service, and an airline.

- At the supermarket the customer can use bonus points to purchase items that can be bought only with bonus points. The customer earns 5 bonus points for any regular purchase greater than $25.
- The gas stations offer a discount of 5% on every bill.
- The car rental service offers 20 bonus points for every $100 spent.
- Customers can save bonus points for free flights with the airline company. For every flight that is paid for normally, the airline offers 1 bonus point for each 15 miles of flight.

In this situation, there are two types of transactions. First, there are transactions in which the customer obtains bonus points. In the model (see Figure 2-1), these transactions are represented by a subclass of *Transaction* called *Earning*. Second, there are transactions in which the customer spends bonus points. In the model they are represented by instances of the *Burning* subclass of *Transaction*. The gas stations offer simple discounts but do not offer or accept bonus points. Because the gas stations do not use bonus points, they do not render transactions on the *LoyaltyAccount*.

Customers in the Silver and Gold program who make extensive use of the membership are rewarded with a higher level of service: the gold card. All normal services are available to customers who have a gold card, and they are also offered additional services.

- Every two months the supermarket offers an item that is completely free: it does not even cost bonus points. The average value of the item is $25.
- The gas stations offer a discount of 10% on every purchase.
- The car rental service offers a larger car for the same price.
- The airline offers its gold card customers a business class trip for the economy class price.

Customers must meet at least one of the following conditions to get a gold card.

- Three sequential years of membership with an average annual turnover of $5,000
- One year of membership with a turnover of $15,000, where the turnover is the total turnover with all program partners

To administer different levels of service, the class *ServiceLevel* is introduced in the model. A service level is defined by the loyalty program and used for each membership.

R&L advertises the program and its conditions. It manages all customer data and transactions on the loyalty accounts. For this purpose, the program partners must inform R&L of all transactions on loyalty program membership cards. Each year, R&L sends new membership cards to all customers. When appropriate, R&L upgrades a membership card to a gold card. In this case, R&L sends the customer a new gold card along with information on the additional services offered, and R&L invalidates the old membership card.

The customer can withdraw from the program by sending a withdrawal form to R&L. Any remaining bonus points are canceled and the card is invalidated. R&L can invalidate a membership when the customer has not used the membership card for a certain period. For the Silver and Gold program, this period is one year.

We could tell you more about R&L, but the preceding description is sufficient for our purposes. We can now add to the model in Figure 2-1 a number of useful and necessary constraints.

2.2 PUTTING INVARIANTS ON ATTRIBUTES

It is simple to put an invariant on one or more attributes of a class. First, you indicate the class on which to put the invariant. This class is called the *context* of the invariant. (In this book, we underline the class name, but this convention is not part of the UML-OCL standard.) Then build a boolean expression that states your invariant. All attributes of the context class may be used in this invariant.

In the R&L example, a reasonable invariant for every loyalty program would be to demand that every customer who enters a loyalty program be of age. In the model, this means that the attribute *age* of every customer object must be equal to or greater than 18. In OCL, this can be written as

```
Customer
age >= 18
```

When the attribute is not of a standard type, such as *Boolean* or *Integer,* but its type is a class itself, you can use the operations defined on that class to write the invariant on the attribute. The operation name and its parameters are written after the attribute name, and the attribute and operation names are separated by a dot. For example, a simple but useful invariant on the date attribute of *CustomerCard* states that *validFrom* should be earlier than *goodThru*:

```
CustomerCard
validFrom.isBefore(goodThru)
```

This invariant uses the operation *isBefore* in the *Date*[1] class that checks whether the date in the parameter is earlier than the date object, and that results in a boolean value.

2.3 PUTTING INVARIANTS ON ASSOCIATED CLASSES

You can put an invariant on attributes of objects of one class (as shown in the preceding section) or on attributes of objects of associated classes, as shown next. In OCL, you can use the *rolename* to refer to the object on the other end of the association. Or, if the rolename is not present, you can use the *classname* starting with a lowercase letter. For R&L, it would be useful to demand that the card and the customer related to a membership are related to each other; that is, a card issued for a membership is in the possession of the customer who is mentioned in the membership. In OCL, this can be stated as

```
Membership
card.customer = customer
```

This invariant literally means that the customer linked to the card object in a membership is the same object as the customer linked to the membership.

Similarly, we can put an invariant on the attributes of associated classes:

```
CustomerCard
printedName = customer.title.concat( customer.name )
```

This invariant means that the attribute *printedName* in every instance of *Customer-Card* must be equal to the concatenation of the *title* and *name* attributes of the associated instance of *Customer*.

2.4 DEALING WITH COLLECTIONS OF OBJECTS

Often the multiplicity of an association is greater than 1, thereby linking one object to a set of objects of the associated class. To deal with such a set, OCL has a number of operations called *collection* operations. Whenever the link in a constraint results in a set of objects, you can use one of the collection operations by putting an arrow between the rolename (or lowercase classname) and the operation. For example, in the loyalty program Silver and Gold, the number of service levels equals 2. The invariant is

---

[1] The *Date* class is not intoduced here but is described in Section 5.3.

```
LoyaltyProgram
serviceLevel->size = 2
```

Another invariant on the R&L model is that the number of valid cards for every customer must be equal to the number of programs the customer participates in. This constraint can be stated using the *select* operation on sets. The *select* takes an OCL expression as parameter. The result of the *select* is a subset of the set on which it is applied, where the parameter expression is true for all elements of the subset. In the following example, the result of the *select* is the subset of *card*, where *card.valid* is true.

```
Customer
program->size = cards->select( valid = true )->size
```

Also relevant for the R&L model is that, when none of the services offered in a *LoyaltyProgram* credits or debits the *LoyaltyAccount* instances, these instances are useless and should not be present. We use the *forAll* operation on the collection of all services to state that all services comply with this condition. The *forAll* operation, like the *select*, takes an expression as parameter. Its outcome is boolean: true if the expression evaluates to true for all elements in the collection, and otherwise false. The following invariant states that when the *LoyaltyProgram* does not have the possibility for earning or burning points, the members of the *LoyaltyProgram* do not have *LoyaltyAccounts*; that is, the collection of *LoyaltyAccounts* associated with the *Memberships* must be empty.

```
LoyaltyProgram
partners.deliveredServices->forAll(
         pointsEarned = 0 and pointsBurned = 0 )
    implies membership.loyaltyAccount->isEmpty
```

This example introduces two logical operations: *and* and *implies*. The *and* operation is the normal *and* operation on booleans. The *implies* operation states that when the first part is true, the second part must also be true; when the first part is not true, it does not matter whether the second part is true.

Some other collection operations are as follows (the complete list can be found in Chapter 3 and Appendix A).

* *notEmpty*, which is true when the set has at least one element
* *includes(object)*, which is true when *object* is an element of the set
* *union(set of objects)*, which results in a set of objects that holds the elements in both sets
* *intersection(set of objects)*, which results in a set of objects that holds all elements that are in both sets

2.4.1 Sets, Bags, and Sequences

When working with collections of objects, you should be aware of the difference between a *set*, a *bag*, and a *sequence*. In a set, each element may occur only once. In a bag, elements may be present more than once. A sequence is a bag in which the elements are ordered. To understand why these differences are important, take a look at the attribute *numberOfCustomers* of class *ProgramPartner*. We want to state that this attribute holds the number of customers who participate in one or more loyalty programs offered by this program partner. In OCL, this would be expressed as

```
ProgramPartner
numberOfCustomers = loyaltyProgram.customer->size
```

But there is a problem with this expression. A customer can participate in more than one loyalty program. In other words, an object of class *Customer* could be repeated in the collection *loyaltyProgram.customer*. So this collection is a bag and not a set. In the preceding expression, these customers are counted twice, and that is not what we intended.

In OCL, the rule is that when you navigate through more than one association with multiplicity greater than 1, you end up with a bag. When you navigate just one such association you get a set. Of course, there are standard operations that transform a set into a bag or sequence, a bag into a set or sequence, or a sequence into a set or bag. Using one of these operations we can correct the previous invariant:

```
ProgramPartner
numberOfCustomers = loyaltyProgram.customer->asSet->size
```

When you navigate an association marked *{ordered}*, the resulting collection is a *Sequence*. Several standard operations deal with the order of a sequence: *first, last,* and *at(index)*. The only ordered association in the R&L model lies between *LoyaltyProgram* and *ServiceLevel*. From the context of *LoyaltyProgram*, the expression *serviceLevel* results in a sequence. We can state that the first element of this sequence must be named *Silver* as follows:

```
LoyaltyProgram
serviceLevel->first.name = 'Silver'
```

2.5 INHERITANCE

The advantage of using inheritance is that an object using superclass instances need not know about the subclasses. But sometimes you want to use the subclasses. In the R&L example, the program partners want to limit the number of bonus points they give away; they have set a maximum of 10,000 points to be burned for each partner. The following constraint sums up all the points of all transactions for a partner. It does not specify our intent because it does not differentiate between burning and earning transactions.

```
LoyaltyProgram
partners.deliveredServices.transaction.points->sum < 10,000
```

To determine the subclass to which an element of this collection of transactions belongs, we use the standard operation *oclType*. To retrieve from the collection all instances of this subclass, we use the *select* operation. We use the *collect* operation to retrieve from the collection of burning transactions a set of points. These are the points that are summed and compared with the given maximum.

```
LoyaltyProgram
partners.deliveredServices.transaction
        ->select(oclType = Burning)
                ->collect( points )->sum < 10,000
```

2.6 WORKING WITH ENUMERATIONS

Sometimes an enumeration type is defined as an attribute type in a UML class model. The values an attribute of this type can hold are indicated in an OCL expression with a # symbol before the valuename. An example can be found in the *CustomerCard* class, where the attribute *color* can have two values, either *silver* or *gold*, as shown earlier in Figure 2-1. The following invariant states that the color of this card must match the service level of the membership.

```
Membership
actualLevel.name = 'Silver' implies card.color = #silver
and
actualLevel.name = 'Gold' implies card.color = #gold
```

2.7 WRITING PRECONDITIONS AND POSTCONDITIONS

In Section 1.2, we described the design by contract principle and the use of pre- and postconditions. Pre- and postconditions specify the effect of an operation without stating an algorithm or implementation. When pre- and postconditions for operations must be precisely defined, OCL is a good tool. To indicate the operation for which the conditions must hold, we extend the constraint context with the name of the operations. This means that all attributes and links from the object in the context can be used, but the expressions following the context declaration must hold for the given operation only.

In the R&L example, the class *LoyaltyAccount* has an operation *isEmpty*.[2] When the number of points on the account is zero, the operation returns the value *true*. To state this more precisely, the operation returns the outcome of the boolean expression *points = 0*. In the following example, the return value of the operation is indicated by the OCL keyword *result*.

```
LoyaltyAccount::isEmpty()
pre : -- none
post: result = (points = 0)
```

There is no precondition for this operation, so we include a comment, "none" where the precondition should be placed. To include a precondition, even if it is an empty one, is not mandatory. Rather, it is a matter of style. If this example were part of a list of operations with their pre- and postconditions and if the precondition for the *isEmpty* operation was the only one missing, the reader might misinterpret its meaning and think that the precondition was missing. In this example, we could have omitted the precondition completely.

2.8 WHERE TO START WRITING INVARIANTS

The class on which the invariant must be put is called the *invariant context*. From the invariant context, you can state an invariant on any object that is linked to the invariant context. Earlier in this chapter, we stated an invariant on the age of a customer:

```
Customer
age >= 18
```

We could have placed the invariant on *LoyaltyProgram* instead of *Customer*:

```
LoyaltyProgram
customer->forAll( age >= 18 )
```

The invariant on *LoyaltyProgram* is a valid constraint, but the invariant on *Customer* is easier to read. In Chapter 4, you can read more about how to choose the right context. For now, just remember that it is good practice to always choose the invariant that is the simplest to write.

---

[2] Note that this operation is different from the *isEmpty* operation defined on sets.

2.9 BROKEN CONSTRAINTS

Note that the OCL expression in a constraint does not tell you what happens when the constraint is broken. One could argue that, because constraints are part of the system's specification, in a correctly implemented system constraints are never broken. A broken constraint invalidates the complete system. Because it is difficult to implement a system correctly, runtime constraint checking is good practice. Obviously, some action will have to be undertaken if a constraint is broken, such as printing a warning or shutting down the system. This form of programming is known as *defensive programming*.

2.10 SUMMARY

In this chapter, we have shown how to write invariants and pre- and postconditions. All these constraints are written in the context of a UML model. Constraints never stand alone.

Constraints specified in OCL are used during modeling or specification and are not an implementation description. They specify what must be true in a perfect, correct implementation. What happens when a constraint is broken in an incorrect (or broken) implementation cannot be specified using OCL.

The OCL description in this chapter is neither complete, nor precisely specified. Chapter 3 and Appendix A give the complete specification of the OCL language.

Chapter 3

The Complete Overview of OCL Constructs

This chapter describes all the constructs with which you can write constraints ranging from simple integer expressions to complex navigations through the associations on a class diagram.

3.1 TYPES AND INSTANCES

The basic building blocks for OCL expressions are objects and object properties. In OCL, each object has a certain type, which defines the operations that can be applied on the object. Types in OCL are divided into the following groups.

- Predefined types, including
  - basic types
  - collection types
- User-defined model types

The predefined basic types are *Integer*, *Real*, *String*, and *Boolean* and are described in this chapter in some detail. Their definition is close to that in many known languages, and Appendix A gives the complete information on these basic types.

The predefined collection types are *Collection*, *Set*, *Bag*, and *Sequence*. They are used to specify the exact results of a navigation through associations in class models. You need to know these types to write more complex expressions.

Model types, such as *Customer* or *LoyaltyProgram*, are defined by the UML models. Each class, interface, or type in a UML model is automatically a type in OCL, including enumeration types that can be used as attribute types.

3.1.1 Value Types and Object Types

OCL has value types and object types. Both are types (that is, both specify instances), but there is an important difference. *Value types* define instances that never change their value. The integer 1, for example, will never change its value and become an integer with a value of 2. *Object types* or classes represent types that define instances that can change their value(s). An instance of the model type *Person* can change the value of its attribute *name* and still remain the same instance. Martin Fowler [Fowler97] calls object types *reference objects* and value types *value objects*.

Another important characteristic of value types is that the value *is* the instance, hence the name. Two occurrences of a value type that have the same value are by definition the same instance. Two occurrences of an object can have the same value or different values. They are the same instance only if they have the same object identity.

Both the predefined basic types and the predefined collection types of OCL are value types. The user-defined model types can be either value types or object types.

3.2 OCL EXPRESSIONS AND OCL CONSTRAINTS

Before getting into the OCL constructs, let us begin by discussing the difference between the expressions that are valid OCL expressions and the OCL expressions that are valid constraints. Any expression can be a valid OCL expression if it is written according to the rules we will explain in this chapter.

> *An OCL expression is valid if and only if it is written according to the rules of OCL.*

Each OCL expression has a type: either a model type (that is, a class or any other type defined in a UML model) or a predefined OCL type. Each OCL expression has a result: the value that results from evaluating the expression. The result of the expression *1+3* is *4*. The type of the result value is the type of the expression—in this case, *Integer*.

In Section 1.1, we defined a constraint to be a restriction on one or more values of (part of) an object-oriented model or system. A constraint is specified using a boolean expression that evaluates to true if the restriction holds. A constraint, then, is a boolean expression, *Boolean* being one of the predefined types. Within OCL, not all expressions have to be of the boolean type: for example, the expression *1+3* is a valid OCL expression of type *Integer*. Therefore, a good definition of an OCL constraint is as follows:

> *An OCL constraint is a valid OCL expression of type Boolean.*

The result value of a constraint is therefore either true or false.

3.3 THE CONTEXT OF AN OCL EXPRESSION

The context of an OCL expression is always a specific element of a UML model. The kind of model element that constitutes the context for a constraint depends on the kind of constraint.

3.3.1 The Context of an Invariant

The context of an invariant is always a class, an interface, or a type. In this book, the convention is to show the type of the model element underlined on the line above the expression, as in the next example.

```
Customer
name = 'Edward'
```

This type is the contextual type, or in short the context. In this book, only one expression follows the context declaration. This is a convention and not part of the standard.

If the OCL expression following the context declaration is used as an invariant, it means that for all instances of the contextual type, the expression must evaluate to true. Thus, in our example, all instances of class *Customer* would have to be named Edward.

3.3.2 The Context of a Pre- or Postcondition

The context of pre- and postconditions is always an operation or a method. The parameters of the contextual operation are accessible in the OCL expression constituting the pre- and postconditions.

The convention used in this book is to show the operation to which a pre- or postcondition applies on a separate line, underlined. The operation is prepended with the class, interface, or type to which it belongs. The complete signature of the operation is shown with all parameters, their types, and the return type of the operation. The information for this complete operation signature is defined in the UML class model. Following this context definition are lines—labeled with *pre*: or *post*:—that contain the actual pre- and postconditions. The general case looks like this:

```
Type1::operation(arg : Type2) : ReturnType
pre : arg.attr = true
post: result = arg.attr xor self.attribute2
```

Only the expressions following the *pre* and *post* labels are OCL expressions. The rest is syntactic sugar according to our conventions for this book.

The contextual type (see preceding section) is the class, interface, or type to which the operation or method belongs. The special *self* keyword refers to the object whose operation will be performed.

3.3.3 The *self* Keyword

Sometimes it is necessary to refer explicitly to the context object. The special name *self* always refers to the context object. The previous expression thus can be written as follows:

```
Customer
self.name = 'Edward'
```

Here is an example of an invariant in which the explicit reference to *self* is needed:

```
Membership
customer.card.membership.includes( self )
```

Whenever the name *self* is used it refers to the instance of the type that is the context of the OCL constraint. If the context is *Customer,* then *self* refers to an instance of *Customer.* We can see *self* as the object from which we start the expression. In most cases, *self* can be omitted because the context is clear:

```
Customer
name = 'Edward'
```

3.4 BASIC TYPES AND OPERATORS

In Chapter 2, we used the type *String* and the operator = assuming that they are familiar to most of our readers. But we have not yet given any definition of the basic predefined types of OCL. In the following sections we will discuss the basic value types and their operations.

Basic types are typically very "basic" and not interesting to read about, so this section is deliberately kept short and explains only the more interesting operations of the basic types. For details on the commonly known operations you are referred to Appendix A, which contains the complete definition of all basic types and their operations from the official UML standard. Still, OCL basic types are not exactly the same as in most programming languages and therefore offer some surprises.

Remember that although OCL expressions are always written within the context of a model and its diagrams, all basic value types are independent of any diagram and can be used in any expression. Just as the expression *1+3* is always a

Table 3-1 *Standard operations for the Boolean type.*

Operation	Notation	Result type
or	a or b	Boolean
and	a and b	Boolean
exclusive or	a xor b	Boolean
negation	not a	Boolean
equals	a = b	Boolean
not equals	a <> b	Boolean
implies	a implies b	Boolean
if then else	if a then b else b' endif	Type of b and b'

valid OCL expression, so the boolean expression *true = not false* is always a valid constraint, independent of the model to which it is applied.

3.4.1 The *Boolean* Type

A *Boolean* can have only one of two values: *true* or *false*. The operations defined on *Boolean* include all the familiar ones, shown in Table 3-1. A standard operation on the *Boolean* type that is uncommon to most programming languages—but often encountered in a more theoretical environment or in specification languages—is the implies operation (denoted by *implies*). This operation states that the result of the total expression is true if it is the case that, when the first *Boolean* operand is true, the second *Boolean* operand is also true. If the first *Boolean* operand is false, the whole *implies* expression always evaluates to true.

Take as an example the class *Service* from the Royal & Loyal example, which is depicted in Figure 3-1. The result of the following sample expression is true if for every service it can be said that when it offers bonus points it never burns bonus points. In other words, a customer cannot earn bonus points when using a service that is bought with bonus points.

```
Services
self.pointsOffered > 0 implies not self.pointsBurned = 0
```

Another interesting operation on the *Boolean* type is the if-then-else. It is denoted in the following manner.

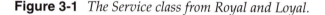

Figure 3-1 *The Service class from Royal and Loyal.*

```
if <boolean OCL expression>
then <OCL expression>
else <OCL expression>
endif
```

The result value of an *if-then-else* operation is the result of either the OCL expression in the *then* clause or the OCL expression in the *else* clause, depending on the result of the boolean expression in the *if* clause. You cannot omit the *else* clause of the expression because an OCL expression must result in a value. Omitting the *else* clause causes the expression to result in an undefined state if the boolean OCL expression in the *if* clause is false. Both OCL expressions within the *else* and the *then* clauses must be of the same type.

Take as an example the *Customer* class shown in Figure 3-2 from the Royal and Loyal model. The following is an invariant constraint on this class.

```
Customer
title = (if isMale = true
            then 'Mr.'
            else 'Ms.'
         endif)
```

This constraint states that for all instances of *Customer* the *title* is 'Mr.' if the attribute *isMale* is true; otherwise the title is 'Ms.'.

Here are some other examples of valid *Boolean* expressions:

```
not true
```

Customer

name : String
title : String
age : Integer
isMale : Boolean

Figure 3-2 *The Customer class from Royal and Loyal.*

```
age() > 21 and age() < 65
age() <= 12 xor cards->size > 3
title = 'Mr.' or title = 'Ms.'
name = 'Foobar'
if standard = 'UML'
   then 'using UML standard'
   else 'watch out: non UML features'
endif
```

3.4.2 The *Integer* and *Real* Types

The *Integer* type in OCL represents the mathematical natural numbers. Because OCL is a modeling language, there are no restrictions on the values of integers; in particular, there is no such thing as a maximum integer value. In the same way, the *Real* type in OCL represents the mathematical concept of real values. As in mathematics, *Integer* is a subtype of *Real*.

For the *Integer* and *Real* types, the usual operations apply: addition, subtraction, multiplication, and division. For both the *Integer* and the *Real* types, there is an additional absolute operator that gives the absolute value of the given value; for example, *1* for *-1.abs* or *2.4* for *(2.4).abs*. An additional operator on the *Real* type is the *floor* operator, which rounds the value of the *Real* down to an integer number; for example, *(4.6).floor* results in an *Integer* instance with the value 4. The *round* operation on a *Real* results in the closest *Integer*; for example, *(4.6).round* results in the *Integer* 5. An overview of all operations on integers and reals is given in Table 3-2. The formal specifications can be found in Appendix A.

The following examples illustrate the *Real* and *Integer* types. All these examples result in true.

```
2654 * 4.3 + 101 = 11513.2
(3.2).floor / 3 = 1
1.175 * (-8.9).abs - 10 = 0.4575
12 > 22.7 = false
12.max(33) = 33
33.max(12) = 33
13.mod(2) = 1
13.div(2) = 6
33.7.min(12) = 12
-24.abs = 24
(-2.4).floor = -3
```

3.4.3 The *String* Type

Strings are sequences of characters. Literal strings are written with enclosing single quotes, such as *'apple'* or *'weird cow'*. The operations available on *Strings* are *toUpper*, *toLower*, *size*, *substring*, and *concat* (see Table 3-3).

Table 3-2 *Standard operations for the Integer and Real types.*

Operation	Notation	Result type
equals	a = b	Boolean
not equals	a <> b	Boolean
less	a < b	Boolean
more	a > b	Boolean
less or equal	a <= b	Boolean
more or equal	a >= b	Boolean
plus	a + b	Integer or Real
minus	a - b	Integer or Real
multiplication	a * b	Integer or Real
division	a / b	Real
modulus	a.mod(b)	Integer
integer division	a.div(b)	Integer
absolute value	a.abs	Integer or Real
maximum of a and b	a.max(b)	Integer or Real
minimum of a and b	a.min(b)	Integer or Real
round	a.round	Integer
floor	a.floor	Integer

Here are some examples to illustrate the *String* type. All these examples result in true.

```
'Anneke'.size = 6
('Anneke' = 'Jos') = false
'Anneke '.concat('and Jos') = 'Anneke and Jos'
'Anneke'.toUpper = 'ANNEKE'
'Anneke'.toLower = 'anneke'
'Anneke and Jos'.substring(12, 14) = 'Jos'
```

Table 3-3 *Standard operations for the String type.*

Operation	Expression	Result type
concatenation	string.concat(string)	String
size	string.size	Integer
to lower case	string.toLower	String
to upper case	string.toUpper	String
substring	string.substring(int,int)	String
equals	string1 = string2	Boolean
not equals	string1 <> string2	Boolean

3.5 MODEL TYPES

As mentioned earlier, constraints are always defined with regard to a certain UML model. The classes, types, interfaces, and datatypes defined in the UML model are, within OCL, considered to be classes of which instances can be made. In other words, all these UML model elements define types within OCL. The developer of the UML model can therefore create new types that are—within the context of the UML model—as valid as any of the OCL predefined types. These newly defined types are called *model types*. We have already used model types many times, but in this section we will describe exactly what a model type is and what *properties* can be used with it. The properties of a model type are

- Attributes
- Operations and methods
- Navigations that are derived from associations (and aggregations)[1]
- Enumerations defined as attribute types

Model types are denoted by the name they have in the UML model, for instance in the class diagram. Valid model types are the types, classes, interfaces, association classes, actors, use cases, and datatypes defined in the UML model. Examples from the R&L model are *Service, ProgramPartner, Customer,* and all other classes as well as the enumeration *{silver, gold}* defined in the *CustomerCard* class. The *Date* class is also a model type. Although it is not completely defined in the class model of Figure 2-1, it is clear that *Date* is an auxiliary class that must be defined else-

---

[1] Of course, inheritance relationships cannot be navigated, because they don't represent relationships between instances.

where in order for the complete model to be consistent. Section 5.3 describes such a *Date* class.

3.5.1 Attributes from the UML Model

If the class *Customer* is specified in the UML model, as in Figure 3-3, then *Customer* is a valid type in OCL. All attributes of *Customer* in the class model are also attributes of *Customer* within OCL.

The attribute *name* of this class, with type *String*, can be used within an OCL expression. The syntax is a dot followed by the attribute name.

```
Customer
self.name
```

This is an expression of type *String*, because the attribute *name* is of type *String*.

3.5.2 Operations from the UML Model

As with attributes, the operations and methods that are defined on the model types in a UML model can be used in OCL. However, there is one fundamental restriction. Because OCL is a side-effect-free language, operations that change the state of any object are not allowed in OCL. Only so-called *query operations*, which return a value but don't change anything, can be used in OCL. In UML, each operation and method has a boolean label called *isQuery*. If this label is true, the operation or method has no side effects. Only these query operations can be used in OCL expressions. Of course, the pre- and postconditions of query operations and methods can still be specified in OCL.

The dot notation used to reference attributes is also used to reference operations. The name of the operation, however, is always followed by two parentheses, which enclose the optional arguments of the operation. Given the class *Customer* defined in Figure 3-3 we can write

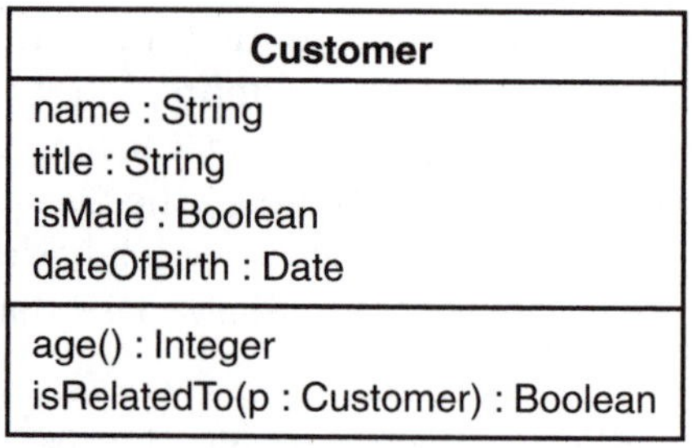

Customer
name : String title : String isMale : Boolean dateOfBirth : Date
age() : Integer isRelatedTo(p : Customer) : Boolean

Figure 3-3 *The Customer class from Royal and Loyal.*

```
Customer
self.age() >= 0

Customer
self.isRelatedTo(self) = true

Customer
self.name = 'Jos senior' implies self.age() > 21
```

As you can see, even if an operation has no arguments, the parentheses are mandatory. This is necessary to distinguish between attributes and operations, because UML allows attributes and operations to have identical names. Figure 3-4, for example, is a correct UML model.

For this class we can write

```
OtherPerson
self.age() > 21 implies self.age = 'mature'
```

Another example from the R&L model is an invariant on the value of the query operation *program()*.

```
Transaction
self.program() = customerCard.membership.program
```

3.5.3 Class Operations and Attributes from the UML Model

*Class operation*s and *class attributes* from the UML model are properties of their corresponding OCL types. Their syntax is identical to the syntax of the normal operations and attributes. For example, in Figure 2-1 the attribute *now* of *Date* is a class attribute. It can be used as follows.

```
Date
Date.now
```

The result of this expression is an object of type *Date*.

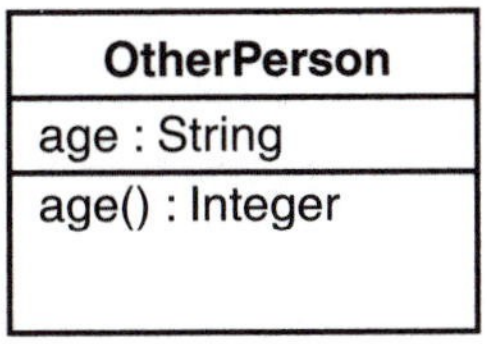

OtherPerson
age : String
age() : Integer

Figure 3-4 *Class with identical attribute and operation names.*

3.5.4 Associations and Aggregations from the UML Model

The third property of a model type from a UML model that we can use within OCL is derived from the *associations* in the class model. For a class or type, each attached association defines a *navigation*: a shift of attention from a class or type to an associated class or type. The name of the navigation is the rolename at the opposite (or "far") end of the association. If a rolename is missing, the name of the navigation is the name of the type (starting with a lowercase letter) at that end of the association. If using the typename results in an ambiguity, the use of a rolename is mandatory.

In Figure 3-5, which is part of the Royal and Loyal model, there are two navigations defined on *Customer*: *program* and *cards*. Class *CustomerCard* has one navigation defined: *owner*. Class *LoyaltyProgram* has one navigation: *customer*.

Navigations are treated as attributes whose types are model types or collections. The dot-notation used to reference attributes is also used to reference navigations. In UML, attribute names and rolenames at the far end of an association cannot be identical. This arrangement prevents ambiguities between attribute and navigation names.

The result type of a navigation is either a model type or a collection of model types. If the multiplicity is at most 1, the result type is a model type; if the multiplicity is higher than 1, the result is a collection. As shown in Figure 3-5, the result type of the *owner* navigation from *CustomerCard* is a model type: *Customer*. The result type of both the navigations *program* and *card* from *Customer* are collections, in this case *Sets*. The result of navigating more than one association with multiplicity *many* is by definition a *Bag*. The difference between bags and sets is described in Section 3.6.

In Figure 3-5 we can use navigation starting with *CustomerCard*:

```
CustomerCard
self.owner
```

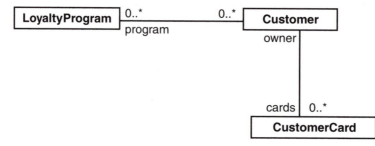

Figure 3-5 *Navigation.*

Because the result of the preceding expression is an instance of type *Customer*, we can use the dot notation to navigate to a set of objects that is associated with the *Customer* instance.

```
CustomerCard
self.owner.program
```

If the multiplicity of the association is greater than 1, the result of the navigation is a *Set* of instances. Thus, the following navigation results in a set of *Customer*s.

```
LoyaltyProgram
self.customer
```

The type of this expression is denoted by *Set(Customer)*. As we said before, a navigation can be viewed as a special kind of attribute. From Figure 3-5 we can derive the following attributes. Note that the following syntax and definitions are not part of OCL itself but are merely used to explain the use and semantics of navigations.
On *CustomerCard*:

```
owner : Customer
```

On *Customer*:

```
cards    : Set(CustomerCard)
program  : Set(LoyaltyProgram)
```

On *LoyaltyProgram*:

```
customer : Set(Customer)
```

When we combine navigations, we have the means to navigate through the complete class diagram. From the context of one class in the class diagram we can write constraints on all connected classes! Surely, this is not good practice. When and how to use the navigation notation is covered in Chapter 4.

3.5.5 Association Classes from the UML Model

A UML class model allows us to define *association classes*, which are classes attached to an association. From an association class you can always navigate to the instances of the classes at all ends of the association. Note that such a navigation always results in one single value and never in a collection of any kind.

In our Royal and Loyal model (see Figure 3-6) we have one such class: *Membership*. The following invariant states that the actual service level of a membership

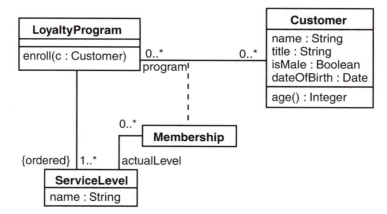

Figure 3-6 *Association class from the UML model.*

must aways be a service level of the loyalty program to which the membership belongs.

```
Membership
program.serviceLevel->includes( actualLevel )
```

It is also possible to navigate in the other direction: from the associated classes to the association class. In the Royal and Loyal model, we can navigate from *Customer* and *LoyaltyProgram* to *Membership*. Because an association class cannot have a rolename, the navigation name is the name of the association class, starting with a lowercase letter. The following invariant makes a statement similar to the preceding one but from the context of the *LoyaltyProgram*: the set of service levels must include the set of all actual levels of all memberships.

```
LoyaltyProgram
serviceLevel->includesAll( membership.actualLevel )
```

Note that navigation to an association class results in a *Set* and not in a single instance.

3.5.6 Qualified Associations from the UML Model

In a UML model you can use *qualified associations*. Qualified associations can be used in OCL expressions in the same way that normal associations are used. The only difference is that we need a way to indicate the value of the qualifier in the expression. The syntax used for qualified associations is

```
object.navigation[qualifierValue, ...]
```

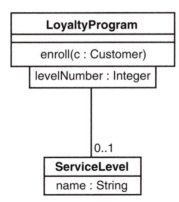

Figure 3-7 *Qualified association in the UML model.*

If there are multiple qualifiers, their values are separated by commas. You can navigate to all associated objects by not specifying a qualifier. This is identical to navigation of normal associations.

Figure 3-7 shows an alternative class model for the R&L model. The ordered association from *LoyaltyProgram* to *ServiceLevel* is replaced by an association with the qualifier *levelNumber*. This means that for each combination of a *LoyaltyProgram* and a *levelNumber* there is one or zero *ServiceLevel*. The *levelNumber* specifies the order of the *ServiceLevels.*

To specify that the name of the *ServiceLevel* with *levelNumber* 1 must be *'basic'*, we can write the following invariant:

```
LoyaltyProgram
self.serviceLevel[1].name = 'basic'
```

If we want to state that there is at least one *ServiceLevel* with the name *'basic'*, disregarding the *levelNumber,* we can state the following invariant:

```
LoyaltyProgram
self.serviceLevel->exists(name = 'basic')
```

The first part, *self.serviceLevel,* is the collection of all *ServiceLevels* associated with the *LoyaltyProgram.* The *exists* operation states that at least one of those service levels must have its *name* attribute equal to *'basic'.*

3.5.7 Using Package Names in Navigations

Another aspect of modeling with UML is the ability to divide a model into different packages. Of course, associations between classes, types, or interfaces in these different packages can be used in OCL expressions. In most cases, the item names used in the various packages are different from one another, and therefore associations between the items in two different packages can be treated in the manner described earlier. If name clashes occur, the item in the second package must be qualified by the package name. The syntax for using a package name is

```
PackageName::roleName
```

This phrase identifies an instance of the class that is identified by *roleName* in the package *PackageName*.

The R&L example is not large enough to make use of packages, but suppose for the sake of the example that the class *ProgramPartner* is part of a package called *PartnerAspects* and the class *LoyaltyProgram* is part of a different package called *ProgramAspects*, as depicted in Figure 3-8.

In this case, the following constraint can be formulated:

```
LoyaltyProgram
self.PartnerAspects::partners->size < 10
```

The meaning of this constraint is simply that the number of program partners is less than 10.

3.5.8 Using Pathnames in Inheritance Relations

The previous sections describe the common way to use properties on objects. When multiple inheritance is used in a class model, properties need not be unique. Different properties with identical names can be inherited from different

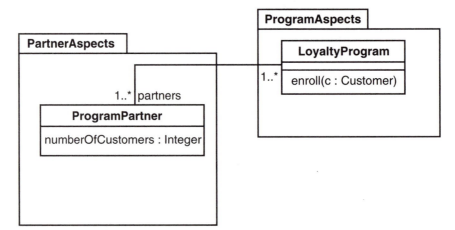

Figure 3-8 *Classes in different packages.*

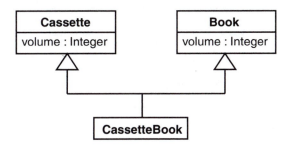

Figure 3-9 *Ambiguity caused by multiple inheritance.*

superclasses. Figure 3-9 shows an example of the class *CassetteBook*, which has two superclasses: *Cassette* and *Book*. The attribute *volume* is inherited twice, with different definitions. For a *Cassette*, *volume* is the strength of the audio signal on the tape. The *volume* of a *Book* is the number that the book has in the series to which it belongs.

The following invariant on *CassetteBook* is ambiguous, because we don't know which of the two *volume* attributes is meant.

```
CassetteBook
self.volume < 10
```

To resolve this ambiguity, we can use the *pathname* construct of OCL. A pathname allows us to prepend a property with the inheritance path. The preceding invariant can be stated as

```
CassetteBook
self.Cassette::volume < 10
```

This shows that the *volume* attribute is the one inherited from *Cassette*.

3.5.9 Enumeration Types

An *enumeration type* is a special model type often used as a type for attributes. It is defined within the UML model by using the enumeration syntax.

```
enum{ value1, value2, value3 }
```

The values defined in the enumeration can be used as values within an OCL expression. To use one of the values in an OCL expression, prefix it with the # symbol.

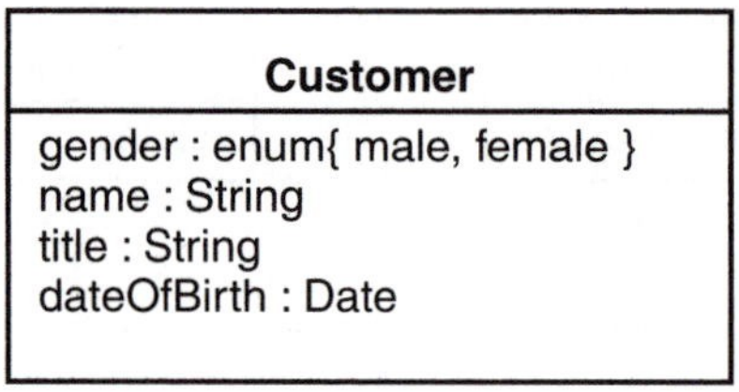

Customer
gender : enum{ male, female } name : String title : String dateOfBirth : Date

Figure 3-10 *Customer class with enumeration.*

In Figure 3-10, the *Customer* class is shown again. Now we have changed the attribute *isMale* to an attribute *gender*. The following invariant states that male *Customer*'s must be approached using the title *'Mr.'*.

```
Customer
gender = #male implies title = 'Mr.'
```

The only operators available on enumeration values are the equality and inequality operators. They are denoted by = and <>, respectively.

3.6 THE SET, BAG, AND SEQUENCE TYPES

In object-oriented systems, the manipulation of collections (of objects) is a very common thing. Because one-to-one associations are rare, most associations define a relationship between one object and a collection of other objects. To let you manipulate these collections, OCL predefines a number of types for dealing with collections, sets, and so on.

Within OCL there are four collection types. Three of them—the *Set*, *Bag*, and *Sequence* types—are concrete types and can be used in constraint definitions. The fourth, the *Collection* type, is the abstract supertype of the other ones and is used to define the operations common to all collection types. In this book, we refer to *Set*, *Bag*, and *Sequence* as the collection types. With these collection types come a large number of predefined operations that manipulate collections in various ways. These operations are explained in the following sections.

All collection types are defined as value types; that is, the value of an instance cannot be changed. Remember that OCL is free of side effects. Therefore, collection operations do not change a collection, but they may result in a new collection. So indeed, instances of collection types do not change their values.

The three concrete collection types are defined as follows:

- A *Set* is a collection that contains instances of a valid OCL type. A *Set* does not contain duplicate elements; any instance can be present only once.

- A *Bag* is like a *Set*, but it can contain duplicate elements; that is, the same instance can occur in a bag more than once. A *Bag* is typically something you get when combining navigations. This concept is introduced in Section 2.4.1 and explained further in Section 3.6.10.
- A *Sequence* is like a *Bag* but the elements are ordered.[2] Elements in a *Bag* or *Set* are not ordered.

In the R&L model, the following expressions result in a collection.

```
LoyaltyProgram
self.customer              -- Set       (Customer)
self.serviceLevel          -- Sequence(ServiceLevel)
```

The following examples result in single instances.

```
Transaction
self.programPartner        -- ProgramPartner
self.card                  -- CustomerCard
```

All operations on collections are denoted in OCL expressions using the arrow notation. This practice makes it easy to distinguish an operation of a model type from an operation on a collection. In the following example, from R&L, the property following the arrow is applied to the collection before the arrow.

The following invariant states that the number of participants in a loyalty program must be less then 10,000.

```
LoyaltyProgram
self.customer->size < 10000
```

Another invariant states that the first service level of a loyalty program is called *'basic'*.

```
LoyaltyProgram
self.serviceLevel->first.name = 'basic'
```

3.6.1 Treating Instances as Collections

Because the OCL syntax for applying collection operations is different from that for model type operations, we can use a single instance as a collection. This collection then is a *Set* with the instance as the only element. For example, in the Royal and Loyal model from Figure 2-1 the following constraint results in the value of the attribute *isEmpty* of an instance of *LoyaltyAccount*.

---

[2] Note that a *Sequence* is ordered and not sorted. Each element has a sequence number, like array elements in programming languages.

```
Membership
loyaltyAccount.isEmpty
```

On the other hand, the following constraint results in the value of the *Set* operation *isEmpty*, where the *LoyaltyAccount* is used as a collection.

```
Membership
loyaltyAccount->isEmpty
```

This constraint evaluates to true if the link from the instance of *Membership* to an instance of *LoyaltyAccount* is empty; that is, the *Membership* has no attached *LoyaltyAccount*.

3.6.2 Flattening Collections

A special feature of OCL collections is that all collections are automatically *flattened*; that is, a collection never contains collections but contains only simple objects. Whenever a collection is inserted into another collection, the resulting collection is automatically flattened; the elements of the inserted collection are considered direct elements of the resulting collection. The reason for this approach is that collections of collections (and deeper) are conceptually difficult and are seldom used in practice. An example is given by the following two collections, which are identical.

```
Set { Set { 1, 2 }, Set { 3, 4 }, Set { 5, 6 } }
Set { 1, 2, 3, 4, 5, 6 }
```

All operations on collection types are clearly and precisely defined in Appendix A. The following sections give a short explanation of the collection operations, but if you have any doubts refer to the appendix for the complete definition.

3.6.3 Operations on All Collection Types

All collection types have the operations shown in Table 3-4 in common. These operations are defined by the supertype *Collection*.

3.6.4 Operations with Variant Meaning

Some operations are defined for all three collection types but have a slightly different, specialized meaning when applied to one type or another.

- The *equals* operator (denoted by =) evaluates to true if all elements in two sets are the same. For two bags to be equal, the number of times an element is present must also be the same. For two sequences, the order of elements must also be the same.

Table 3-4 *Standard operations on all collection types.*

Operation	Description
size	The number of elements in the collection.
count(object)	The number of occurrences of object in the collection.
includes(object)	True if the object is an element of the collection.
includesAll(collection)	True if all elements of the parameter collection are present in the current collection.
isEmpty	True if the collection contains no elements.
notEmpty	True if the collection contains one or more elements.
iterate(expression)	Expression is evaluated for every element in the collection. The result type depends on the expression.
sum()	The addition of all elements in the collection. The elements must be of a type supporting addition (such as Real, Integer).
exists(expression)	True if expression is true for at least one element in the collection.
forAll(expression)	True if for all elements expression is true.

- The *union* operation combines two collections into a new one. The union operation is also defined to combine a set with a bag (and vice versa), but a sequence may not be combined with either a set or a bag, only with another sequence.
- The *including* operation adds one element to the collection. For a bag, this description is completely true. If the collection is a set, then the element is added only if it is not already present in the set. If the collection is a sequence, the element is added at the end.
- The *excluding* operation removes an element from the collection. From a set, it removes only one element. From a bag or sequence, it removes all occurrences of the given object.
- The *intersection* operation results in another collection that contains the elements that are in both collections. This operation is valid for combinations of

two sets, a set and a bag, or two bags, but not for combinations involving a sequence.

Following are examples of the use of the *includes* and *includesAll* operations. In the following invariant we specify that the actual service level of a membership must be one of the service levels of the program to which the membership belongs.

```
Membership
program.serviceLevel->includes(actualLevel)
```

The following example is an invariant which specifies that the available services for a service level must be offered by a partner of the loyalty program to which the service level belongs.

```
ServiceLevel
loyaltyProgram.partners
                ->includesAll(availableServices.programPartner)
```

3.6.5 Operations for the *Set* Type

There are two operations defined only for the *Set* value type: minus (denoted by -) and *symmetricDifference*.

- The *minus* operation results in a new Set that contains all elements that are in the first set but not in the second set.
- The *symmetricDifference* operation results in a set that contains all elements that are in the first or in the second set but not in both.

Here are some examples:

```
Set{1,4,7,10} - Set{4,7} = Set{1,10}
Set{1,4,7,10}.symmetricDifference(Set{4,5,7}) = Set{1,5,10}
```

3.6.6 Operations for the *Sequence* Type

All the operations that are defined only for the *Sequence* value type have to do with the ordering of a sequence.

- The *first* and *last* operations result in the first and the last elements of the sequence, respectively.
- The *at* operation results in the element at the given position.
- The *append* and *prepend* operations add an element to a sequence as the last or first element, respectively.

Here are some examples:

```
Sequence{1,4,7,10}->first = 1
```

```
Sequence{1,4,7,10}->last = 10
Sequence{1,4,7,10}->at( 3 ) = 7
Sequence{1,4,7,10}->append( 15 ) = Sequence{1,4,7,10,15}
Sequence{1,4,7,10}->prepend( 15 ) = Sequence{15,1,4,7,10}
```

3.6.7 Operations That Iterate over Collection Elements

OCL has a number of standard operations that allow you to handle the elements in a collection: *select*, *reject*, *collect*, *iterate*, *forAll*, and *exists*. These operations take each element and evaluate an expression on them. The *select*, *reject*, and *collect* operations result in a new collection, whereas *forAll* and *exists* result in a *Boolean*. The result of the *iterate* operation depends on its arguments. The following sections explain each of these operations in more detail.

3.6.8 The *select* Operation

Sometimes an expression using operations and navigations results in a collection, but we are interested only in a special subset of the collection. The *select* operation is a special operation on a collection that allows us to specify a selection from the original collection. The result of the *select* operation is always a subset of the original collection.

The parameter of the *select* operation is a boolean expression that specifies which elements we want to select from the collection. The result of the *select* is the collection that contains all elements for which the boolean expression is true. The following expression selects all transactions on a *CustomerCard* that have more than 100 *points*.

```
CustomerCard
self.transactions->select( points > 100 )
```

Within the *select*, the context for the boolean expression is an element of the collection on which the *select* operation is invoked.

We can explain the meaning of the *select* operation in an operational way, but the *select* is still an operation without side effects; it results in a new set. The result of *select* can be described by the following pseudocode:

```
element = collection.firstElement();
while( collection.notEmpty() ) do
    if( <expression-with-element> )
    then
        result.add(element);
    endif
    element = collection.nextElement();
endwhile
return result;
```

When the *select* is evaluated, *element* iterates over the *collection* and the *expression-with-element* is evaluated for each *element*. If this evaluates to true, the *element* is included in the *result* set.

The syntax of the *select* operation comes in three different forms:

```
collection->select( element : Type | <expression> )
collection->select( element | <expression> )
collection->select( <expression> )
```

The first form is the most comprehensive syntax. It declares an *iterator variable* called *element*. The type of this iterator variable is declared as *Type*. The result of the *select* is the collection that consists of each element in collection for which *<expression>* results in true. For example, consider this expression:

```
Customer
membership.loyaltyAccount->select(a : LoyaltyAccount |
                                        a.points > 0)
```

It results in the collection of all accounts that have a positive number of points.

The second form is a shorthand notation, in which the type of the iterator variable is omitted. The type is deduced from the type of elements in the original collection. The meaning of the expression is identical to that of the long form. The following example is the same as the preceding one:

```
Customer
membership.loyaltyAccount->select(a | a.points > 0)
```

The third form, the shortest one, does not define an iterator variable. It omits all syntactic sugar and is therefore often the easiest one to read and write. The following example is the same as the preceding ones:

```
Customer
membership.loyaltyAccount->select( points > 0 )
```

The *points* attribute is now taken in the context of a *LoyaltyAccount*. This context is not explicit, as in the longer form, but it is implicit. This works in the same way as the reference to *self* that can be omitted and become implicit.

The shortest form cannot be used in some circumstances. It can be used only if an explicit reference to the iterator is not needed in the expression. For example, the following expression cannot be rewritten in the short form because of the reference to the iterator:

```
ProgramPartner
self.loyaltyProgram.partners->
```

```
select(p : ProgramPartner | p <> self)
```

This expression results in the collection of all program partners that are in the same loyalty programs as the context program partner.

3.6.9 The *reject* Operation

The *reject* operation is analogous to the *select*, with the distinction that the *reject* selects all elements from the collection for which the expression evaluates to false. The following two expressions are equivalent:

```
c->reject(e : Type | <expression>)
c->select(e : Type | not <expression>)
```

The following two invariants are semantically equivalent:

```
Customer
membership.loyaltyAccount->select( points > 0 )
```

```
Customer
membership.loyaltyAccount->reject( not (points > 0) )
```

The *reject* operation has the same three syntax forms as *select*. The existence of *reject* is merely a convenience.

3.6.10 The *collect* Operation

The *collect* operation iterates over the collection, computes a value for each element of the collection, and gathers the evaluated values into a new collection. The type of the elements in the resulting collection is usually different from the type of the elements in the collection on which the operation is applied. The following expression represents a collection of *Integer* values collected from the values of the *point* attribute in *Transaction*.

```
LoyaltyAccount
transaction->collect( points )
```

We can use this expression to state a constraint on this collection of *Integer* values. For example, we could demand that at least one of the values must be 500.

```
LoyaltyAccount
transaction->collect( points )->
                    exists( p : Integer | p = 500 )
```

The result of the *collect* operation on a *Set* or *Bag* is a *Bag*; on a *Sequence* the result is a *Sequence*. Like *select* and *reject*, the *collect* operation has three possible syntax forms:

```
collection->collect( element : Type | <expression>)
collection->collect( element | <expression> )
collection->collect( <expression> )
```

3.6.11 Shorthand Notation for *collect*

Because the *collect* operation is used extensively, a shorthand notation has been introduced. This shorthand can be used only when there can be no misinterpretations. Instead of the preceding constraint, we can write

```
LoyaltyAccount
transactions.points->exist(p : Integer | p = 500 )
```

In this expression, *transactions* is a set of *Transactions*; therefore, only the set properties can be used on it. The notation *transactions.points* is shorthand for *transactions->collect(points)*. Thus, when we take a property of a collection using a dot, this is interpreted as taking the property on all elements in the collection and collecting their values in a new collection, as defined by the *collect* operation.

3.6.12 The *forAll* Operation

Many times we want to specify that a certain condition must hold for all elements of a collection. The *forAll* operation on collections can be used for this purpose. The *forAll* operation has the same syntactical variants as *select* and *collect*:

```
collection->forAll( element : Type | <expression>)
collection->forAll( element | <expression> )
collection->forAll( <expression> )
```

The result of the *forAll* operation is a *Boolean*. It is true if the expression is true for all elements of the collection. If the expression is false for one or more elements in the collection, then *forAll* results in false. For example, consider these expressions in the context of a company:

```
LoyaltyProgram
self.customer->forAll( c : Customer | c.age() <= 70 )

LoyaltyProgram
self.customer->forAll( c | c.age() <= 70 )
```

```
LoyaltyProgram
self.customer->forAll( age() <= 70 )
```

These expressions evaluate to true if the age of all participants in a loyalty program is less than or equal to 70. If the age of at least one (or more) customers exceeds 70, the result is false.

The *forAll* operation has an extended variant in which multiple iterators can be declared. All iterators iterate over the complete collection. Effectively, this is a short notation for a nested *forAll* expression on the collection.

```
LoyaltyProgram
self.customer->forAll(c1, c2 | c1 <> c2 implies c1.name <> c2.name)
```

This expression evaluates to true if the names of all customers of a loyalty program are different. It is semantically equivalent to the following expression, which uses nested *forAll* operations:

```
LoyaltyProgram
self.customer->forAll( c1 | self.customer->forAll( c2 |
                        c1 <> c2 implies c1.name <> c2.name ))
```

Although the number of iterators is unrestricted, more than two iterators are seldom used. The multiple iterators are allowed only with the *forAll* operation and not with any other operation that uses iterators.

3.6.13 The *exists* Operation

Often, we want to specify that there is at least one object in a collection for which a certain condition holds. The *exists* operation on collections can be used for this purpose. The *exists* operation has the same syntactical variants as *select* and *collect*:

```
collection->exists( element : Type | <expression> )
collection->exists( element | <expression> )
collection->exists( <expression> )
```

The result of the *exists* operation is a *Boolean*. It is true if the expression is true for at least one element of the collection. If the expression is false for all elements in the collection, then the *exists* operation results in false. For example, in the context of a *LoyaltyAccount* we can state that if the attribute *points* is greater than zero, there exists a *Transaction* with *points* greater than zero.

```
LoyaltyAccount
points > 0 implies transaction->exists(points > 0)
```

Obviously, there is a relationship between the *exists* and the *forAll* operations. The following two expressions are equivalent.

```
collection->exists( <expression> )

not collection->forAll( not < expression> )
```

3.6.14 The *iterate* Operation

The *iterate* operation is the most fundamental and complex of the collection operations. At the same time, it is very generic. The *select, reject, collect, forAll,* and *exists* operations can all be described as a special case of *iterate,* as shown in Appendix A.

The syntax of the *iterate* operation is as follows:

```
collection->iterate( element : Type1;
                     result  : Type2 = <expression>
              | <expression-with-element-and-result>)
```

The variable *element* is the iterator. The resulting value is accumulated in the variable *result,* which is also called the accumulator. The accumulator gets an initial value *<expression>.*

The result of the *iterate* operation is a value accumulated by iterating over all elements in a collection. We can define the *iterate* operation using the following pseudocode.

```
result = <expression>;
while( collection.notEmpty() ) do
    element = collection.nextElement();
    result  = <expression-with-element-and-result>;
endwhile
return result;
```

When the *iterate* is evaluated, *element* iterates over the *collection* and the *expression-with-element-and-result* is evaluated for each *element.* After each evaluation of *expression-with-element-and-result,* its value is assigned to *result.* In this way the value of *result* is built up during the iteration of the collection.

An example of the *iterate* operation can be found in the R&L model. Suppose that every program partner wants to restrict the number of points burned by all its customers: the number of points burned may never exceed the number of points earned. First, we accumulate for a *ProgramPartner* all transactions: *self.services.transaction.* Then we differentiate between the two subclasses of *Transaction:* the *Burning* and the *Earning* classes. (This can easily be done using the *oclType* operation, which returns the class of the instance and is explained in detail in Section 3.8.) We then use the *iterate* operation to add up the number of points for all

Burning instances and repeat the process for all *Earning* instances. Finally, we compare the two sums and state the constraint using a simple comparison operation (<=) defined on the standard *Integer* type.

```
ProgramPartner
self.services.transaction->iterate(
    t      : Transaction;
    result : Integer = 0 |
    if t.oclType = Burning then
        result + points
    else
        result
    endif
)
<=
self.services.transaction->iterate(
    t      : Transaction;
    result : Integer = 0 |
    if t.oclType = Earning then
        result + points
    else
        result
    endif
)
```

In this case, the result of the *iterate* operation is of the *Integer* type, so we could have used the *sum* operation defined on *Integer*s. The *sum* operation is a shortcut for the specific use of the *iterate* operation, as is shown by its definition in Appendix A.

```
ProgramPartner
self.services.transaction->select(oclType = Burning)->sum
<=
self.services.transaction->select(oclType = Earning)->sum
```

3.7 CONSTRUCTS FOR POSTCONDITIONS

On the one hand, we can use operations in constraints; on the other hand, we can write constraints for operations. There are two ways to write constraints for operations: preconditions and postconditions. In postconditions we use two special keywords that represent, to some extent, the working of time: *result* and *@pre*.

The @ symbol followed by the *pre* keyword indicates the value of an attribute or association at the start of the execution of the operation. The keyword must be postfixed to the name of the item concerned, as shown in the following example.

```
LoyaltyProgram::enroll(c : Customer)
pre : not customer->includes(c)
post: customer = customer@pre->including(c)
```

The precondition states that the customer to be enrolled is not already a member of the program. The postcondition states that the set of customers after the enroll operation is identical to the set of customers before the operation with the enrolled customer added to it. We could also add a second postcondition stating that the membership for the new customer owns a loyalty account with zero points and no transactions.

```
post: membership->select(customer = c)->forAll(
        loyaltyAccount->notEmpty() and
        loyaltyAccount.points = 0   and
        loyaltyAccount.transactions->isEmpty )
```

The keyword *result* indicates the return value from the operation. The type of *result* is defined by the return type of the operation. In the following example, the type of *result* is *LoyaltyProgram*.

```
Transaction::program():LoyaltyProgram
post: result = self.card.membership.program
```

In this example, the result of the program operation is the loyalty program against which the transaction was made. The *self.card* is the *CustomerCard* associated with the transaction, and *self.card.membership* is the membership to which this customer card belongs. The *self.card.membership.program* is the loyalty program to which the membership belongs.

3.8 OPERATIONS DEFINED ON EVERY OCL TYPE

A number of operations are useful for every type of OCL instance. These operations are described in Sections A.1.1 and A.1.2.

Within the OCL context, the type *OclAny* is defined as the supertype of all types in the model. All model types inherit the properties of *OclAny*; that is, properties defined for *OclAny* are available for each object in an OCL expression. To avoid name conflicts between properties from the model and the properties inherited from *OclAny*, all names of the properties of *OclAny* start with *ocl*. Although theoretically there may still be name conflicts, you can avoid them by not using the *ocl* prefix in the class model. You can also use the pathname construct (see Section 3.5.8) to refer to the *OclAny* properties explicitly. For a full description of *OclAny*, see Section A.1.2.

Table 3-5 *Operations on any OCL instance.*

Expression	Result type
object = (object2 : OclAny)	Boolean
object <> (object2 : OclAny)	Boolean
object.oclType	OclType
object.oclIsKindOf(type : OclType)	Boolean
object.oclIsTypeOf(type : OclType)	Boolean
object.oclAsType(type : OclType)	Type

The type of any OCL instance is an instance of *OclType*, which allows you access to the meta-level of the model. This access can be useful for advanced modelers. The operations defined for all OCL objects are shown in Table 3-5.

The *oclIsTypeOf* operation is true only if the type of the object is identical to the argument. The *oclIsKindOf* operation is true of the type if the object is identical to the argument or identical to any of the subtypes of the argument. The operation *oclType* simply returns the type of the object. The operation *oclAsType* results in the same *object* but of type *type*. This operation can be used to re-type objects when their type is known but the deduced type in the OCL expression is one of its supertypes. If the actual type of *object* is not equal to *type*, the result is *Undefined*.

The following examples, which are based on Figure 3-11 show the difference between the *oclIsKindOf* and *oclIsTypeOf* operations. For a *Transaction*, the following invariants are valid:

```
Transaction
self.oclType = Transaction
self.oclIsKindOf(Transaction) = true
self.oclIsTypeOf(Transaction) = true
```

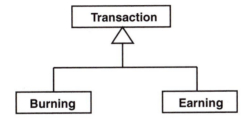

Figure 3-11 *Difference between oclIsKindOf and oclIsTypeOf.*

```
self.oclIsTypeOf(Burning) = false
self.oclIsKindOf(Burning) = false
```

For the subclass *Burning,* the following invariants are valid:

```
Burning
self.oclType = Burning
self.oclIsKindOf(Transaction) = true
self.oclIsTypeOf(Transaction) = false
self.oclIsTypeOf(Burning) = true
self.oclIsKindOf(Burning) = true
self.oclIsTypeOf(Earning) = false
self.oclIsKindOf(Earning) = false
```

The *oclIsKindOf, oclIsTypeOf,* and *oclType* operations are often used to specify invariants on subclasses. For example, Figure 3-12 shows a general association between *FruitPie* and *PieceOfFruit.* For the different subtypes of *FruitPie,* only specific subtypes of *PieceOfFruit* are acceptable.

Using *oclType* or one of the other operations, we can state the invariants for the subtypes of *FruitPie: ApplePie* and *PeachPie.*

```
ApplePie
self.ingredient->forAll(oclIsKindOf(Apple))
```

```
PeachPie
self.ingredient->forAll(oclIsKindOf(Peach))
```

Chapter 4 elaborates on this usage and the consequences.

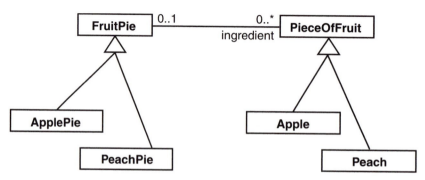

Figure 3-12 *Invariants on subtypes.*

3.9 TYPES AS OBJECTS

In OCL it is possible to access the meta-level. At the meta-level, a type itself is an instance of *OclType*. This arrangement allows us to use properties defined on the type itself instead of properties of the instances only. A number of properties on types are defined by OCL. They can be found in Table 3-6, where *sometype* represents a type (such as *Customer* or *Membership*). The class attributes and class operations defined in the UML model are also properties of the corresponding model types in OCL.

The *name* is the name of *sometype* as a *String*. The *attributes, associationEnds*, and *operations* are sets of the names of, respectively, the attributes, association ends, and operations defined for *sometype*. The attribute *supertypes* is the set of all direct supertypes of *sometype*. The attribute *allSupertypes* is the set of all direct supertypes of *sometype*, including their supertypes, recursively, until there is no supertype. Following are some examples of these operations:

```
Customer.name = 'Customer'

Transaction.attributes = Set('points', 'date')

Transaction.associationEnds =
          Set{'serviceLevel', 'loyaltyAccount', 'card'}

Burning.supertypes = Set{ Transaction }

Transaction.operations = Set{'program'}
```

Table 3-6 *Properties on types.*

Expression	Result
sometype.name	String
sometype.attributes	Set(String)
sometype.associationEnds	Set(String)
sometype.operations	Set(String)
sometype.supertypes	Set(OclType)
sometype.allSupertypes	Set(OclType)
sometype.allInstances	Set(sometype.oclType)

The property *allInstances* results in a set of all instances of a type, including all instances of its subtypes. The following expression results in the set of all instances of type *Transaction*, including all instances of type *Burning* and *Earning*.

```
Transaction.allInstances
```

As mentioned earlier class attributes and class operations defined in the class model are properties of their type in OCL, just as attributes and operations are properties of instances in OCL. For example, the class operation *now*, as defined on *Date* in Figure 2-1, can be used in OCL as follows.

```
Date.now        -- results in a Date instance
```

3.10 TYPE CONFORMANCE RULES

OCL is a typed language. When you are constructing a new expression from other expressions, the subexpressions and the operator must "fit." If they don't, the expression is invalid, and the parser will complain that the expression contains a type conformance error. The definition of *conformance* that is used within OCL is as follows:

> *Type1 conforms to Type2 if an instance of Type1 can be substituted at each place where an instance of Type2 is expected.*

Here are the type conformance rules:

- *Type1* conforms to *Type2* when they are identical.
- *Type1* conforms to *Type2* when *Type1* is a subtype of *Type2*.
- Each type is a subtype of *OclAny*.
- Type conformance is transitive; that is, if *Type1* conforms to *Type2* and *Type2* conforms to *Type3*, then *Type1* conforms to *Type3*. Together with the first rule, this means that a type conforms to any of its predecessors in an inheritance tree.
- *Integer* is a subtype of *Real* and therefore conforms to *Real*.

In addition to the preceding type conformance rules, the following rules are defined for the collection types:

- Every type *Collection(T)* is a subtype of *OclAny*. The types *Set(T)*, *Bag(T)*, and *Sequence(T)* are all subtypes of *Collection(T)*.
- *Collection(Type1)* conforms to *Collection(Type2)* if *Type1* conforms to *Type2*.
- *Set(T)* does not conform to *Bag(T)* or *Sequence(T)*.
- *Bag(T)* does not conform to *Set(T)* or *Sequence(T)*.
- *Sequence(T)* does not conform to *Set(T)* or *Bag(T)*.

For example, in Figure 3-12, *PeachPie* and *ApplePie* are two separate subtypes of *FruitPie*. In this example the following statements are true.

- *Set(ApplePie)* conforms to *Set(FruitPie)*.
- *Set(ApplePie)* conforms to *Collection(ApplePie)*.
- *Set(ApplePie)* conforms to *Collection(FruitPie)*.
- *Set(ApplePie)* does not conform to *Bag(ApplePie)*.
- *Bag(ApplePie)* does not conform to *Set(ApplePie)*.
- *Set(AppePie)* does not conform to *Set(PeachPie)*.

3.11 PRECEDENCE RULES

When so many operations are available on an instance of a type, rules are needed to determine the precedence of the operations. The precedence rules for OCL canbe deduced from the formal grammar in Appendix B. Table 3-7 shows the OCL operations, starting with the highest precedence. In case of doubt, the use of parentheses () is always allowed to specify the precedence explicitly.

3.12 COMMENTS

OCL expressions can contain *comments*. An OCL comment begins with two hyphens. All text from the hyphens to the end of the line, is considered to be a comment. For example, the following lines contain *valid* OCL expressions:

Table 3-7 *Precedence for OCL operations (highest to lowest).*

Name	Syntax
Pathname	::
Time expression	@pre
The dot and arrow operations	., ->
Unary operations	-, not
Multiplication and division	*, /
Addition and substraction	+, -
Relational operations	<, >, <=, >=, <>, =
Logical operations	and, or, xor
Logical implies	implies

```
-- the expression 20 * 5 + 4 should be evaluated here
20 * 5 + 4 -- this is a comment
```

The following line is *not a valid* OCL expression:

```
20 * -- this is a comment 5 + 4
```

3.13 UNDEFINED

An OCL expression may result in *Undefined*. An example of an undefined expression is an attempt to take the attribute value of a nonexisting object. Any OCL expression in which part of the expression is undefined, is undefined as a whole. There are a few exceptions:

- If one of the arguments of the *Boolean or* is true, the whole *or* is true even if the other argument is undefined. Thus, *Undefined or true* and *true or Undefined* are both true.
- If one of the arguments of the *Boolean and* is false, the whole *and* is false even if the other argument is undefined. Thus, *Undefined and false* and *false and Undefined* are both false.

3.14 SUMMARY

In this chapter we have shown the full OCL language. In OCL we can use predefined types, with special emphasis on the various collection types and their operations, Aas well as all types from the UML class model. We have also shown how all information from the UML class model is reflected in OCL. This includes attributes, operations, methods, associations, aggregations, generalizations, association classes, and packages.

Modeling with Constraints

The previous chapters explain the OCL language and describe how to write constraints. This chapter provides guidelines on the many ways in which constraints can be used as a modeling aid and discusses the sometimes subtle differences between them.

4.1 CONSTRAINTS IN A UML MODEL

OCL constraints are always connected to an object-oriented model: either a UML model or some other type of object-oriented model. In a UML model, constraints can be used at various places. This section discusses and defines the various uses of constraints in a UML model.

4.1.1 Invariants

An *invariant* is a constraint that can be associated with a class (including association classes), a type, or an interface in a UML model. An invariant means that the result of the expression must be true for all instances of the associated class or type or interface at any moment in time. This kind of constraint can, for example, put limits on the value of an attribute or link, or it can state that the set of objects in one association must be a subset of those in another association.

The context of an invariant is an object of the associated class, type, or interface. The associated object is also called the contextual object, or the context. The OCL expression that constitutes the constraint is evaluated from the perspective of this contextual object. The standard UML stereotype <<*invariant*>> can be used to indicate an invariant constraint. In a class model, a constraint can be shown as text between curly brackets in a note box with a dotted line to the associated class or type or interface, as shown in Figure 4-1.

Quite often, invariants are not shown on the class model because they take up too much space and they clutter the diagram. This is especially true when the con-

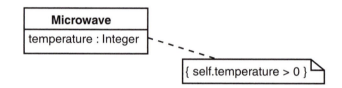

Figure 4-1 *Invariant shown as a note.*

straints become larger or when a large number of constraints are defined for a class model. Invariants can easily be described textually in a separate, or linked, text document. As explained before, in "Typeface Conventions" on page xx of this book indicates the context of a constraint by putting the type of the contextual object first, on a separate line, underlined. The invariant constraints follow on the next line. The invariant from Figure 4-1 can be written in a separate document as

```
Microwave
self.temperature > 0
```

4.1.2 Invariants for Derived Attributes or Associations

A constraint on derived model elements gives information about the relation between the derived element and the element(s) on which it is based. In other words, it states a way to derive the value of the derived element from the base element(s). This derivation can be captured in an invariant expression. This is a special case of the invariant on the class model.

4.1.3 Preconditions and Postconditions

An effective way to specify the semantics of operations and methods is the use of pre- and postconditions (see Chapter 1). A precondition is a constraint that must be true at the start of the execution of the operation. A postcondition must be true at the end of the execution of the operation. Within UML, we can use OCL expressions to specify the pre- and postconditions of operations and methods on all classes, types, and interfaces. The standard UML stereotypes *<<precondition>>* and *<<postcondition>>* are defined for these types of constraints.

In the visual UML class model, there is no specific way to show pre- and postconditions with an operation or method. As with the invariant constraints, you can put the pre- and postconditions in a note box attached to the operation, but this severely clutters the class model,[1] as shown in Figure 4-2. The figure contains one invariant and two very simple postconditions.

---

[1] Tools might provide a fill-in form for an operation, where the pre- and postconditions can be filled in.

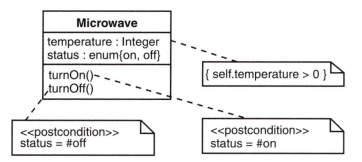

Figure 4-2 *Visual notation for pre- and postconditions.*

The convention used in this book is to show on a separate line, underlined, the operation to which a pre- or postcondition applies. Following this context definition are lines, labeled with *pre:* or *post:*, that contain the actual pre- and postconditions. The general case looks like this:

```
Type1::operation(arg : Type2) : ReturnType
pre : arg.attr = true
post: result = arg.attr xor self.attribute2
```

4.1.4 Guards in State Transition Diagrams

A *transition* can have an event, a guard, and an action. A *guard* on a transition in a state transition diagram is a boolean expression that determines whether or not the transaction is enabled. In other words, the transition takes place only when the guard is true at the moment that the event occurs. A guard is, in fact, a kind of precondition on the transition. A guard is another kind of constraint that can be expressed in OCL.

The state transition model specifies the behavior of one class, and this class is the context for the OCL expression. The guard expression is written in terms of parameters of the event that triggers the transition and in terms of the attributes and links of the object that is specified by the state transition model. An example can be found in the *Bottle* class, as defined in Figure 4-3.

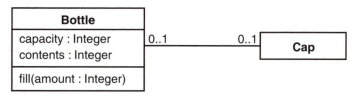

Figure 4-3 *Bottle and Cap classes.*

The attribute *capacity* is the maximum amount that the bottle can hold; *contents* is the amount that the bottle currently holds. The operation *fill* puts the *amount* in the bottle. The behavior of this class is specified by the state transition diagram in Figure 4-4. A bottle can be in four states. The *empty, partially filled,* and *filled* states are used to model the amount of contents in the bottle. In the *capped* state, the bottle is filled and capped.

4.1.5 Using Guards and Events in Pre- and Postconditions

The information in a state transition diagram of a class can be rewritten in the form of pre- and postconditions on operations of that class. This technique can be useful when you are translating the information in the model to an implementation. Events often correspond to operation calls. The state transition diagram tells us when these calls are permitted, which guards must be true, and in what state the object must be to perform this operation. This information on state and guards can be used as preconditions for the operation.

From the state transition diagram you can conclude the effects of an event: the object may enter a different state. This state information can also be included in postconditions.

As an example, consider the state transition diagram for the *Bottle* class in Figure 4-4. Only two events are defined: *fill(amount: Integer)* and *cap.* The *fill* event will undoubtedly be translated into an operation in the implementation code. The precondition for this operation can be read from the state transition diagram: the only state in which the *fill* operation will not perform is *filled*. The postcondition is somewhat more complex. Either the object is in the state *partiallyFilled* and the

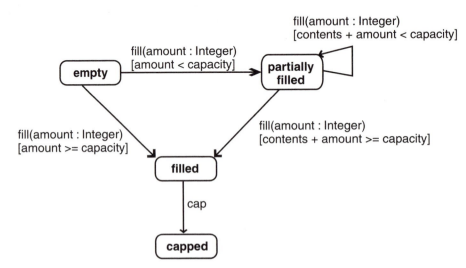

Figure 4-4 *State transition diagram for Bottle.*

new *contents* is less than the *capacity,* or the object is in the state *filled* and the new *contents* is equal to or more than the *capacity.* In OCL, we can express the information from the state transition diagram as follows:

```
Bottle::fill(amount : Integer)
pre: not filled and not capped
post: (partiallyFilled and
                contents@pre + amount < capacity )
       or
       (filled and contents@pre + amount >= capacity )
```

Note that all state names are transformed into attributes of the *Boolean* type. We could have transformed the state names into one attribute of an *Enumeration* type, *state: enum{empty, partiallyFilled, filled, capped},* as in Figure 4-5. In that case, the OCL expressions would be

```
Bottle::fill(amount : Integer)
pre : not state = #filled and not state = #capped
post: (state = #partiallyFilled and
                contents@pre + amount < capacity )
       or
       (state = #filled and
                contents@pre + amount >= capacity )
```

The pre- and postconditions for the *cap* operation are simple:

```
Bottle::cap()
pre : state = #filled
post: state = #capped
```

4.1.6 Change Events in State Transition Diagrams

A *change event* is an event that is generated when one or more attributes or associations change value according to an expression. The event occurs whenever the value of the expression changes from false to true. Note that this is different from

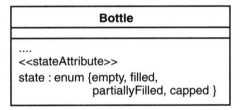

Figure 4-5 *The state attribute.*

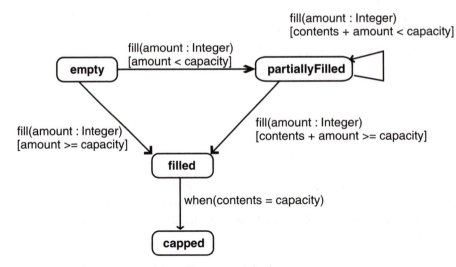

Figure 4-6 *Bottle state transition diagram with change event.*

a guard condition. A guard condition is evaluated once when its event fires; if it is false, the transition does not occur and the event is lost. When a change event occurs, a guard can still block any transition that would otherwise be triggered by that change. A change event is denoted by the keyword *when*, followed by the expression.

In the state transition diagram of the *Bottle* class in Figure 4-4, we can replace the normal *cap* event with a change event. The semantics of this new state transition diagram, as shown in Figure 4-6, are slightly different from the semantics of the former diagram. The *cap* event is an event that must be generated by an object when the bottle is in the *filled* state. The *when* event, however, takes place as soon as the condition *contents = capacity* becomes true. No externally generated event is needed.

The condition of the change event that goes with the *when* can be written in OCL. Of course, the class specified by the state transition diagram is the context of the OCL expression.

4.1.7 Type Invariants for Stereotypes

Stereotypes are new in UML, so the use of type invariants for stereotypes is also new. An invariant on a stereotype is interpreted as an invariant on all types on which the stereotype is applied. The UML meta-model, as described in [UML97], is the class model in which the invariant must be interpreted. Adding a stereotype with a constraint is identical to adding a new meta-class to UML, with the invariant as the well-formedness rule of the new meta-class. Figure 4-7 shows a part of

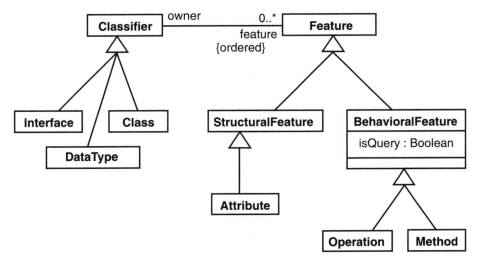

Figure 4-7 *Part of the UML meta-model.*

the UML meta-model, which indicates that a *Classifier* may have *Feature*s. Both *Classifier* and *Feature* have several subclasses.

Stereotypes can be used to specialize UML. This technique is useful if you want to use a modeling concept in UML that is not exactly in UML itself. For example, if you want to state that a class is a value type (see Section 3.1.1), you can define a stereotype *<<valueType>>* on the meta-class *Class*. Whenever a class in a UML model gets this stereotype attached to it, it is a value type. Being a value type means that objects of the type cannot change their values. A restriction for classes with this stereotype is that all operations must be query operations; that is, the meta-attribute *isQuery* must be true for all operations of the class. This can be specified with an OCL invariant on the stereotype *<<valueType>>*:

```
ValueType
self.feature->select(oclIsKindOf(BehavioralFeature))
                   ->forAll( isQuery = true )
```

In this constraint *Class*, *feature*, *BehavioralFeature*, and *isQuery* are all elements defined in the UML meta-model. When you take all features of a class with stereotype *<<valueType>>* and then select all features that are *BehavioralFeature*s, you get the collection of all operations and methods of the class. For each of these, the *isQuery* attribute must be true.

In the R&L model, there is a note stating in natural language that *Date* is a utility class. Giving *Date* the stereotype *<<valueType>>* will state more precisely what we mean, as shown in Figure 4-8.

```
┌─────────────────────────────────┐
│          <<valueType>>          │
│             Date                │
├─────────────────────────────────┤
│ $now : Date                     │
│ isBefore(t : Date) : Boolean    │
│ isAfter(t : Date) : Boolean     │
│ = (t : Date) : Boolean          │
└─────────────────────────────────┘
```

Figure 4-8 *Stereotype for class Date.*

This states that all operations and methods defined for class *Date* are query operations.

4.1.8 Where OCL Expressions Can Be Used

At any location within a UML model, an OCL expression can be used to specify a condition or a specific object or set of objects. The following list shows a number of places where OCL expressions can be used.

- A message in a sequence or collaboration diagram can have an attached condition that specifies in what circumstances the message is sent. This condition can be written as an OCL expression.
- Messages in collaboration and sequence diagrams can take parameters. You can readily specify the value of such a parameter using an OCL expression.
- A transition in a state transition diagram can be coupled to an action. This action is a procedural expression that is executed if and when the transaction fires and is targeted at a specific object or set of objects. An OCL expression can be used to identify the target object or set of objects.

This list is not exhaustive, and we encourage you to find other places where OCL expressions can be used.

4.1.9 Constraints and Inheritance

There are no explicit rules in the UML standard to indicate whether or not a constraint on a superclass is inherited by its subclasses. To use constraints in a meaningful way in an inheritance situation, we need to give them proper semantics. The most accepted semantics is to ensure that any instance of a subclass must behave the same as any instance of its supertype—as far as anyone or any program using the superclass can tell. This principle, called Liskov's Substitution Principle [Liskov94], is defined as follows:

> *Wherever an instance of a class is expected, one can always substitute an instance of any of its subclasses.*

This section describes the consequences for invariants, preconditions, and post-conditions.

The invariants put on the use of the superclass must always apply to the sub-class; otherwise, the substitution principle cannot be safely applied. The subclass may strengthen the invariant, because then the superclass invariant will always hold as well. The general rule for invariants is as follows:

> *An invariant for a superclass is inherited by its subclasses. A sub-class may strengthen the invariant but cannot weaken it.*

In the model in Figure 4-9, we can define for the superclass *Stove* the invariant that its temperature must not be hotter than 200 degrees Celsius.

```
Stove
temperature <= 200
```

It would be dangerous if a subclass *ElectricStove* could exceed that maximum. For example, suppose that *ElectricStove* could have a temperature no hotter than 300 degrees Celsius:

```
ElectricStove
temperature <= 300
```

ElectricStove cannot be used safely in some places where *Stove* can be used. If I have a location that is fire-safe up to 250 degrees Celsius, I know I can safely put a *Stove* there. If I place a *Stove* at this location and if the *Stove* happens to be an *ElectricStove*, the place may be set on fire—definitely not a good idea.

Under some circumstances Liskov's Substitution Principle looks too restrictive. Subclasses may change superclass operations and add their own attributes and operations. The superclass invariants should be changed in correspondence with

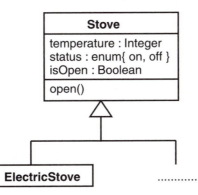

Figure 4-9 *Inheritance of invariants.*

these alterations. Take again the *Stove* example. If the invariant on the temperature is put on the *Stove* because its surroundings would catch fire if the temperature was too high, then a new subclass cannot weaken the invariant. If, on the other hand, the invariant is put on the *Stove* because of the materials used in the construction, then a new subclass might use more fireproof materials. Thus, using the subclass would be safer, even when the invariant on the temperature is weakened. In this case, we recommend rewriting the temperature invariant so that it includes information about the materials used to construct the stove. This approach states the intention of the invariant more cleanly and removes the need to redefine it for each subclass.

When an operation is redefined in a subclass, the question is whether the pre- and postconditions of the original operation in the superclass are inherited. To find the answer, we view the pre- and postconditions as the contract for the operation (see Section 1.2). The design by contract principle follows Liskov's Substitution Principle. The rules for pre- and postconditions are as follows:

> *A precondition may be weakened, not strengthened, in a redefinition of an operation in a subclass.*

> *A postcondition may be strengthened, not weakened, in a redefinition of an operation in a subclass.*

To illustrate these rules, we take the following example. We define the operation *open()* for *Stove* as follows:

```
Stove::open()
pre : status = #off
post: status = #off and isOpen
```

This means that we expect to be able to open a *Stove* when its status is *off*. After we have opened the stove, we expect its status to be *off* and *isOpen* to be true. For *ElectricStove*, we now redefine *open()* and give it different pre- and postconditions:

```
ElectricStove()
pre : temperature <= 100
post: isOpen
```

The precondition of the redefined *open()* includes the *temperature <= 100* constraint. The consequence is that *ElectricStove* does not behave like a *Stove* anymore, because it won't be able to open under the conditions that a *Stove* will open (*status = #off*). If we want to make sure that an *ElectricStove* can be substituted for a *Stove*, the precondition for the redefined *open()* cannot be strengthened. We could weaken the precondition, because it will still work as expected under the conditions for *Stove*.

The postcondition of *open()* in *ElectricStove* is weakened, because the constraint *status = #off* has been removed. The consequence is that the *ElectricStove* won't fulfill the expectations of a *Stove*. After opening, the stove should have *status = #off*. We could have strengthened the postcondition because the original expectation would still be met.

You should follow the rules in this section, because Liskov's Substitution Principle allows safe use of subclasses. Breaking this principle means living dangerously.

4.2 STYLES FOR SPECIFYING CONSTRAINTS

The preceding section descibes the various positions of constraints in UML models. There are also various styles of specifying constraints. How should a certain restriction to the model be expressed? Which placement of the restriction is the most effective? This section gives you guidelines to answer these questions.

4.2.1 Avoiding Complex Navigation Expressions

Using OCL, we can write long and complex expressions that navigate through the complete object model. We could write all invariants on a class model starting from only one contextual type, but that does not mean that it is good practice to do so.

Any navigation that traverses the whole class model creates a coupling between the objects involved. One of the essential notions within object orientation is encapsulation. Using a long navigation makes details of distant objects known to the object where we started the navigation. If possible, we would like to limit the object's knowledge to only its direct surroundings, which are the properties of the type, as described in Section 3.5.

Another argument against complex navigation expressions is that writing, reading, and understanding invariants becomes very difficult. It is hard to find the appropriate invariants for a specific class, and maintaining the invariants when the model changes becomes a nightmare.

Consider the following expression, which specifies that a *Membership* does not have a *loyaltyAccount* if you cannot earn points in the program.

```
Membership
program.partners.deliveredServices->
    forAll(pointsEarned = 0) implies loyaltyAccount->isEmpty
```

Instead of navigating such a long way, we might want to split this. First, we define a new attribute *isSaving* for *LoyaltyProgram*. This attribute is true if points can be earned in the program. The value of *isSaving* can be derived, and we state this as an invariant:

```
LoyaltyProgram
isSaving = partners.deliveredServices->forAll(pointsEarned = 0)
```

The invariant for *Membership* can use the new attribute rather than navigate through the model. The new invariant looks much simpler:

```
Membership
program.isSaving implies loyaltyAccount->isEmpty
```

The *isSaving* attribute can be added to the *LoyaltyProgram* class as an extra OCL attribute, as described in Section 4.2.5.

4.2.2 Choice of Context Object

By definition, invariants apply to a class, type, or interface, so it is important to attach an invariant to the right class. There are no strict rules that can be applied in all circumstances, but some guidelines will help.

- If the invariant restricts the value of an attribute of one class, the class containing the attribute is a clear candidate.
- If the invariant restricts the value of attributes of more than one class, the classes containing any of the attributes are candidates.
- If a class can be appointed the responsibility for maintaining the constraint, that class should be the context. (This guideline uses the notion of responsibility-driven design [Wirfs-Brock90].)
- Any invariant should navigate through the smallest possible number of associations.

Sometimes it is a good exercise to describe the same invariant using different classes as context. The constraint that is the easiest to read and write is the best one to use. Attaching a constraint to the wrong context makes it more difficult to specify and more difficult to maintain.

As an example, let's write an invariant in several ways. The invariant is written for the model in Figure 4-10 and states the following: Two persons who are married to each other are not allowed to work at the same company. This can be expressed as follows, taking *Person* as the contextual object:

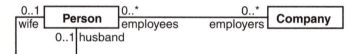

Figure 4-10 *Persons working for companies.*

```
Person
wife.employers->intersection(self.employers)->isEmpty
and
husband.employers->intersection(self.employers)->isEmpty
```

This constraint states that the intersection of the set of employers of the wife or husband of the person with the set of employers of the person, must be empty. This constraint can also be written in the context of *Company*, and that creates a simpler expression:

```
Company
employees.wife->intersection(self.employees)->isEmpty
```

In this example the object that is responsible for maintaining the requirement will probably be the *Company*. Therefore, *Company* is the best candidate context for attaching the invariant.

4.2.3 Use of *allInstances*

The *allInstances* predefined operation on any modeling element results in the set of all instances of the modeling element and all its subtypes. An invariant that is attached to a class always applies to all instances of the class. Therefore, you can often use a simple expression as invariant instead of using the *allInstances* predefined operation. For example, the following two invariants on *Person* are equivalent.

```
Person
Person.allInstances->forAll(p | p.parents->size <= 2)
```

```
Person
parents->size <= 2
```

The use of *allInstances* is discouraged, because it makes the invariant more complex. As you can see from the example, it hides the actual invariant.

4.2.4 Splitting *and* Constraints

Constraints are used during modeling, and they should be as easy to read and write as possible. People tend to write long constraints. For example, all invariants on a class can be expressed in one large invariant, or all preconditions on an operation can be written as one constraint. In general, it is much better to split a complicated constraint into several separate constraints. It is possible to split an invariant at many boolean *and* operations. For example, we can write an invariant for *ProgramPartner* as

```
ProgramPartner
partners.deliveredServices->forAll(pointsEarned = 0)
and
membership.card->forAll(goodThru = Date.fromYMD(2000,1,1))
and
customer->forAll(age() > 55)
```

This invariant is completely valid and useful, but we can rewrite it as three separate invariants, making it easier to read.

```
ProgramPartner
partners.deliveredServices->forAll(pointsEarned = 0)
```

```
ProgramPartner
membership.card->forAll(goodThru = Date.fromYMD(2000,1,1))
```

```
ProgramPartner
customer->forAll(age() > 55)
```

The advantages of this splitting approach are considerable.

- Each invariant becomes less complex and therefore easier to read and write.
- When you are discussing whether an invariant is appropriate, the discussion can be more focused and precise on the invariant concerned, instead of having to deal with the large invariant as a whole.
- When you are checking and finding broken constraints in an implementation, it can point more precisely to the part that is broken. In general, the simpler the invariant, the more localized the problem.
- The same holds true for pre- and postconditions. When a precondition is broken during execution, the problem can be pinpointed much more effectively when you are using small separate constraints.
- Maintaining simpler invariants is easier. If you need to change one condition, then you need change only one small invariant.

4.2.5 Adding Extra Operations or Attributes

It is sometimes useful to define for a class extra query operations or attributes, which you can then use in OCL expressions. Section 4.2.1 shows an example that uses an extra attribute to avoid a complex constraint. Figure 4-11 shows an example that uses an extra query operation. An OCL expression can be used as the

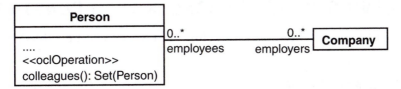

Figure 4-11 *Class with stereotype <<oclOperation>>*

postcondition constraint to specify the result of the operation. The stereotype *<<oclOperation>>* can be defined and attached to such an operation to declare two things about the operation:

- The operation is added to the model for the purpose of using it in OCL expressions.
- The operation does not need to appear in any implementation of the model. It is used for specification purposes only.

The postcondition of the *colleagues()* operation in Figure 4-11 could be

```
Person::colleagues() : Set(Person)
post: result = self.employers.employees->asSet->excluding(self)
```

Often, these extra operations are also useful for other purposes. In that case, they might become normal operations.

4.2.6 Using the *collect* Shorthand

The shorthand for the *collect* operation on collections, as defined in Section 3.6.10, has been developed to streamline the process of reading navigations through the class model. You can read from left to right without the distracting *collect* operations. We recommend that you use this shorthand whenever possible.

For example:

```
Person
self.parents.brothers.children
```

This is much easier to read than

```
Person
self.parents->collect(brothers)->collect(children)
```

Both invariants are identical, but the first one is easier to understand.

4.3 SOLVING MODELING ISSUES WITH CONSTRAINTS

This section focuses on common modeling issues that can be solved using OCL constraints.

4.3.1 Abstract Classes

In a class model, a class can be defined to be *abstract*. If a class X is abstract, this can be defined by the following invariant:

```
X
X.allInstances->select(oclType = X)->isEmpty
```

In the R&L example, the class *Transaction* will likely be an abstract class. Each transaction will be either a *Burning* or an *Earning* transaction.

```
Transaction
Transaction.allInstances->select(oclType = Transaction)->isEmpty
```

4.3.2 Specifying Uniqueness Constraints

A *uniqueness constraint* on an attribute of a class can be described by a simple invariant. Assume that we have a class *Person* with an attribute *socialSecurityNumber* (see Figure 4-12).

The Social Security number must be unique for each instance of *Person*. This is specified using the invariant

```
Person
Person.allInstances->forAll(p1, p2 |
        p1 <> p2 implies p1.socialSecurityNumber <>
                            p2.socialSecurityNumber)
```

Or alternatively you can write the invariant as follows:

```
Person
Person.allInstances->forAll(p |
        p <> self implies p.socialSecurityNumber <>
                            self.socialSecurityNumber)
```

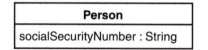

Figure 4-12 *Uniqueness constraint.*

4.3.3 Adding Details to the Model versus Adding Constraints

During modeling, we often encounter situations in which we add detail to the class model to specify the real-world situation precisely. For example, suppose we have a simple class model of a guitar, in which a guitar has a number of guitar strings. Furthermore, there are two types of guitars: electric and classic. We also have two types of guitar strings. Each guitar type has its own kind of guitar strings. This situation is modeled in Figure 4-13.

The association between *Guitar* and *GuitarString* specifies that a *Guitar* has *GuitarString*s. The association between *ClassicGuitar* and *PlasticString* is a redefinition of the same association, which constrains a *ClassicGuitar* to have *PlasticString*s only. The generalization between the associations shows that the lower association is a specialization of the upper, more general association. The association between *ElectricGuitar* and *MetalString* is also a redefinition of the top association.

As you can see, the model becomes comparatively complex. The visual model can be simplified using invariants. The two specializations of the upper association can be captured in two invariants on the two types of guitars, as in the class model shown in Figure 4-14. The visual class model becomes more readable, while the level of detail is retained. The invariants are

```
ClassicGuitar
strings->forAll(oclType = PlasticString)
```

```
ElectricGuitar
strings->forAll(oclType = MetalString)
```

The preceding model can be simplified even more by removing the subclasses of *Guitar*, *GuitarString*, or both. If the main reason for having the subclasses is to dis-

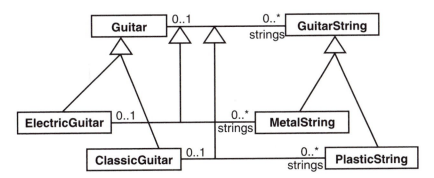

Figure 4-13 *Fully visual model with specializations.*

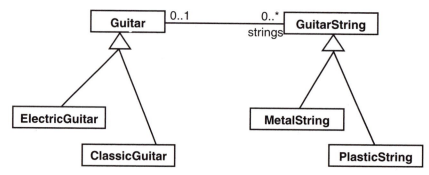

Figure 4-14 *Class model without specialized associations.*

Guitar	0..1	0..*	GuitarString
type : {electric, classic}		strings	type : {plastic, metal}

Figure 4-16 *Class model without subclasses.*

tinguish between different kinds of strings for different guitars, this simplification makes sense. Depending on the situation, this simplification may result in either Figure 4-15 or Figure 4-16.

Here are the invariants for the class model in Figure 4-15:

```
ClassicGuitar
strings->forAll(type = #plastic)


ElectricGuitar
strings->forAll(type = #metal )
```

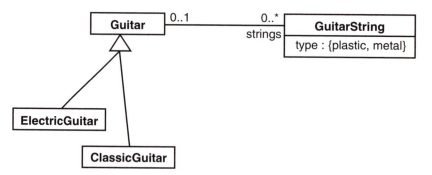

Figure 4-15 *Class model simplified.*

Here are the invariants for the class model in Figure 4-16:

```
Guitar
type = #classic implies strings->forAll(type = #plastic)
```

```
Guitar
type = #electric implies strings->forAll(type = #metal )
```

The deciding question in the trade-off that must be made in these circumstances is which of the solutions will be best in your situation. Figure 4-16 keeps the class model simple, because there is no need for subclasses. If there are no attributes or behavior specific to the subclasses, this is a good solution. In Figure 4-15, we have a more elaborate class model that is suitable when there are attributes or operations specific to the different subclasses. In Figure 4-13, we have an elaborate class model with probably too much detail. This option is desirable if you want to show all details in the visual class model. In general, graphical or visual modeling is best for giving a good overview, whereas textual modeling is good for adding detail. The art is to find the right balance, and that depends on the intended use of the model and the intended audience.

4.3.4 Cycles in Class Models

In many class models, there are *cycles* in the sense that you can start at a class, navigate through various associations, and come back to the same class. Quite often there are restrictions on these cycles. Figure 4-17 shows such a class model with a cycle. In this class model, a *Person* owns a *House*, which is paid for by taking a *Mortgage*. The *Mortgage* takes as security the *House* that is owned by the *Person*.

Although the model looks correct at first glance, it contains an error. Or better stated, it is an imprecise and incomplete model that can give rise to ambiguous specifications. The model allows a person to have a mortgage that takes as security a house that is owned by another person. Expressed in OCL, it can be the case that

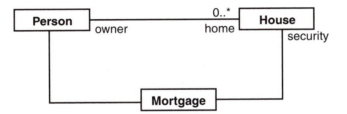

Figure 4-17 *A cycle in a class model.*

```
Person
self.mortgage.security.owner <> self
```

This is clearly not the intention of the model. We can easily state the invariant as

```
Person
self.mortgage.security.owner = self
```

Whenever the multiplicities in a cycle are not equal to zero, we need to take care in writing the invariant. In general, cycles in a class model should be checked carefully, and any constraints on these cycles should be stated as an invariant on one of the classes in the cycle.

4.3.5 Constraints on Associations

A number of constraints on associations are usually shown in the class model. For example, the multiplicity shown in a class model is identical to an invariant on the class at the opposite side of the association. Constraints such as {or} and {subset} are also common in class models.

In the following examples, note that constraints on associations are specified as invariants on one (or more) of the classes involved in the association.

4.3.6 Multiplicity Constraints

In the class model in Figure 4-18, you see a number of multiplicities attached to the associations. The multiplicities are equivalent to the following invariants on the classes involved:

```
Week
self.day->size = 7
```

```
Day
self.week->size = 1
```

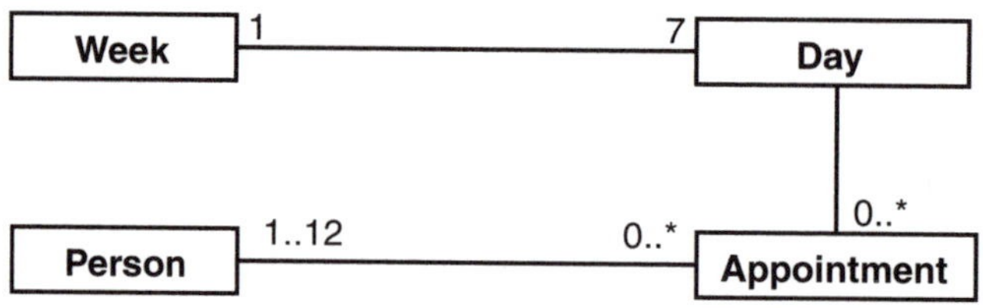

Figure 4-18 *Multiplicity constraints.*

```
Appointment
self.day->size = 1
```

```
Appointment
self.person->size >= 1 and self.person->size <= 12
```

As you can see, each multiplicity is equivalent to a constraint on the size of the collection resulting from navigating the association. The only multiplicity that does not need a constraint is the *0..** multiplicity, because it imposes no restriction at all on the size of the collection.

4.3.7 The Subset Constraint

The model in Figure 4-19 shows several *subset constraints* between two associations. The meaning of this constraint is that the set of links for one association is a subset of the set of links for the other association. In Figure 4-19, *flightAttendants* is a subset of *crew*. The singleton set *pilot* is also a subset of *crew*.

The two subset constraints shown in Figure 4-19 are identical to the following invariants on *Flight*:

```
Flight
self.crew->includes(self.pilot)
```

```
Flight
self.crew->includesAll(self.flightAttendants)
```

4.3.8 The Or Constraint

An *or constraint* between two associations is shown in Figure 4-20. The meaning of this constraint is that only one of the potential associations can be instantiated at one time for any single object. This is shown as a dashed line connecting two or more associations (all of which must have a class in common) with the constraint

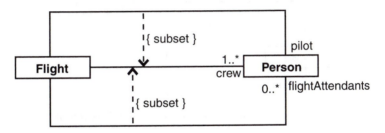

Figure 4-19 *A subset constraint.*

string *{or}* labeling the dashed line. The multiplicity of the associations must be optional, otherwise they cannot be empty.

Figure 4-20 shows an or constraint on two associations. The meaning is that a *House* can have a *Cellar* or a *Basement*, but it can't have both at the same time. The or constraint on the associations is identical to the invariant:

```
House
self.cellar->size + self.basement->size <= 1
```

Or alternatively:

```
House
self.cellar->isEmpty or self.basement->isEmpty
```

Or alternatively:

```
House
self.cellar->notEmpty xor self.basement->notEmpty
```

Note that the visual or constraint is ambiguous in certain situations. This is the case when we have two associations between the same two classes with the multiplicity optional at both ends of both associations. The visual or constraint can now be read in two directions. Figure 4-21 shows an example of this ambiguity.

The visual or constraint on the association can now be interpreted in two directions. In one direction it can mean that one person has either a managed project or a performed project, but not both. In the other direction it can mean that one project has either a project leader or a project member, but not both. Therefore, two different interpretations are possible. Here is the first one:

```
Person
managedProject->isEmpty or performedProject->isEmpty
```

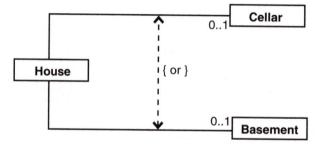

Figure 4-20 *An or constraint.*

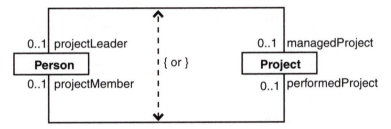

Figure 4-21 *Ambiguous or constraint.*

The second interpretation is:

```
Project
projectLeader->isEmpty or projectMember->isEmpty
```

Although the choice of interpretation may seem obvious in this case, you can imagine the consequences if someone takes the wrong interpretation. Specifying the visual or constraint as an OCL constraint resolves the ambiguity problem. This example shows the importance of formal constraints and illustrates how they ensure that a model is unambiguous.

4.3.9 Optional Multiplicity in Associations

An *optional multiplicity* in a class model is often only a partial specification of what is really intended. Sometimes the optionality is free; that is, in all circumstances there can be either one or no associated object. An example of such an optional association is shown in Figure 4-22. The *Television* may or may not have a *Remote-Control* regardless of the state of the *Television*.

Quite often, an optional association is not really free. Whether an associated object can or must be there depends on the state of the objects involved. For example, in Figure 4-23, the optional association is not completely free. If the attribute *hasFixedControl* is false, there must be a *RemoteControl*. If *hasFixedControl* is true, the link with *RemoteControl* is optional. This constraint can be specified by the following invariant:

Figure 4-22 *Free optional multiplicity.*

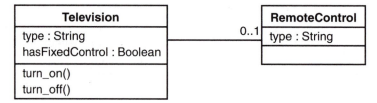

Figure 4-23 *Optional multiplicity.*

```
Television
not hasFixedControl implies remoteControl->notEmpty
```

In general, we can use OCL invariants to describe precisely the circumstances under which optional associations must be empty or not empty.

4.4 SUMMARY

In this chapter, we have shown where to use constraints within the various UML diagrams. As with any specification technique, there are different styles and different ways of expressing the same information. This chapter has shown some of the possibilities and their consequences, focusing on good style. From this chapter you have learned that it is important to give attention to the way you express a constraint, because it has a large impact on readability, maintainability, and the complexity of the associated diagrams.

Chapter 5

Extending OCL

OCL is a language that can be used in many places for many purposes. This book describes OCL as it is defined in the UML standard, but even in the period of time it took to develop this standard, people were asking for extensions to OCL. In the coming years we expect to see new fields in which OCL is used and to receive many requests for extending OCL. We encourage you to experiment with extensions, so this chapter gives some hints and highlights some areas in which extending OCL may be useful.

OCL has been adopted by the OMG as part of the UML standard, so further development is managed by the OMG. Official requests for clarification, changes, bug fixes, and so on can be sent to the OMG. Any request of this kind can also be sent to the authors of this book, who are in direct contact with the OMG concerning OCL.

5.1 A WORD OF CAUTION

OCL is a simple language and does not contain many of the features that are defined in other specification or programming languages. During the development of OCL, we constantly received requests to add specific constructs. Although we have complied with some of these requests, many others have been rejected to retain one of the principles behind OCL: keep it simple.

As summarized in Chapter 1, the requirements for OCL are as follows.

1. OCL must be a language that can express extra (necessary) information on the models.
2. OCL must be a precise, unambiguous language that can be read and written easily.
3. OCL must be a declarative language. Its expressions can have no side effects.
4. OCL must be a typed language.

Although in this chapter we relax the third requirement, the other requirements are still valid for any extension of OCL. Extensions must be typed constructs that are easy to read and write, and they must not complicate the use of constructs that are already part of OCL.

Note that even though we encourage you to extend OCL, until these extensions are accepted into the standard by the OMG, they are your personal property. You must expect problems (for example, in parsing) when using tools based on the OMG standard or when exchanging your OCL expressions with other developers.

5.2 EXTENDING THE STANDARD OCL TYPES

The set of operations on the standard OCL types defined in the UML standard provides all commonly used operations and several basic operations that can be used as building blocks. Any OCL user can add new operations to these standard types, defining them in exactly the same way as the operations in the standard. Describe the name and parameters and specify the pre- and post-conditions. If possible, define the new operation in terms of existing operations. The meaning of the new operation is then built on the standard operations. The *iterate* operation can be particularly helpful in building new operations on collections.

When you add new operations to the standard types, you should consider some consequences.

- New operations on noncollection types must use the dot notation; otherwise, their syntax will not conform to the OCL syntax. Using dot notation ensures that the new operations are parsed correctly.
- New operations on collection types must use the arrow notation; otherwise, their syntax will not conform to the OCL syntax. Using arrow notation ensures that the new operations are parsed correctly.
- New operations are not part of the standard OCL, so tools implementing OCL may treat them as illegal operations. Tools often let you turn off checking or otherwise allow you to add new operations.
- New operations are not standardized and therefore lack portability.

5.3 ADDING NEW OCL TYPES

You cannot add new basic types to OCL, but you can define a new type in a UML model and use it as if it were a basic type. The class, including all its attributes and operations, is defined in the UML model. Such classes and types are often called *utility* classes. Typically, they are imported from a library, which can be project- or company-specific, and are used as the type of an attribute in the class models.

If a number of types are used often in different projects, they can be defined in a separate package that is reused between projects. Each project imports the package.

OCL can easily be extended with different kinds of general-purpose packages. As a simple example, we have defined a package with three classes that represent time and points in time (see Figure 5-1). The granularity in this package is one day. Extending the package to support a smaller granularity is straightforward. Although this example does not include a precise specification of this package with pre- and postconditions in OCL, we recommend that you make this additional effort in real projects.

All classes in the package are value types, so instances don't have identity. See Section 3.1.1

- *Date* is the value type for an absolute point in time. The precision is one day; this means that hours, minutes, and so on cannot be represented by *Date*.

Date
$now : Date year : Integer month : Integer day : Integer
$fromYMD(year, month, day : Integer) : Date plus(d : Duration) : Date minus(d : Duration) : Date isBefore(t : Date) : Boolean isAfter(t : Date) : Boolean periodUntil(t : Date) : Period between(t : Date) : Duration addYear(i : Integer) : Date addMonth(i : Integer) : Date addDay(i : Integer) : Date = (t : Date) : Boolean

Period
start : Date end : Date duration : Duration
$fromTo(t1, t2 : Date) : Period isBefore(p : Period) : Boolean overlaps(p : Period) : Boolean includes(t : Date) : Boolean

Duration
nrOfYears : Integer nrOfMonths : Integer nrOfDays : Integer
$fromDays(days : Integer) : Duration periodBefore(t : Date) : Period periodAfter(t : Date) : Period plus(d : Duration) : Duration minus(d : Duration) : Duration < (d : Duration) : Boolean > (d : Duration) : Boolean = (d : Duration) : Boolean

Figure 5-1 *The Date package.*

- *Duration* is the value type for a length of time. The precision of the duration is in days.
- *Period* is the value type for a period of time determined by two *Date*s, a start date and an end date.

If there is a need to define standard packages, such as the Date/Period/Duration package, then packages might be put forward to the OMG for standardization or they might be registered and published through some other registration means. Because OCL is an OMG standard, this process is probably best coordinated by the OMG.

Using the technique described in this section, you can achieve the effect of adding new types to OCL without altering the OCL language itself. No special features are needed to support new types inside OCL. This arrangement serves one of the requirements of OCL—namely, to stay simple.

5.4 OPERATIONAL USE OF CONSTRAINTS

As described in Section 2.9, a correctly implemented system will never break a constraint. In many practical situations, however, the need will arise to implement the constraints in a running system. In doing this you will encounter many questions, such as how to generate code, when to check constraints, and what to do when a constraint is broken. OCL is a pure modeling language and does not take runtime issues into account.

This section describes some of the problems that you will encounter when implementing constraints in a runtime software system and offers some solutions that may help you in your projects. Remember that this process is not defined in OCL, so you must make the decisions.

5.4.1 Generating Code for Constraints

To use constraints at runtime, you first need to create executable code that checks each constraint. You can do this by using tools that support code generation from OCL or by manually implementing the constraints. In either case, several problems emerge.

Because evaluation order is not (and does not need to be) defined in OCL, it is perfectly legal to write a constraint and have part of that constraint be *Undefined*. What happens when such a constraint is executed in a programming language? For example, consider the following invariant in the R&L model.

```
Membership
loyaltyAccount.points >= 0 or loyaltyAccount->isEmpty
```

If there is no *loyaltyAccount*, the *loyaltyAccount.points* is *Undefined* and the *loyaltyAccount->isEmpty* evaluates to true. In OCL, the result of the whole invariant is true and is well defined. However, if we generate code directly from the invariant, and the execution order is left to right, the *loyaltyAccount.points* code will try to reference a nonexisting object (*loyaltyAccount*). Usually this leads to a runtime error, so care must be taken to avoid such situations.

Another point is that an OCL constraint must always be treated as an atomic expression. No changes of value of any object in the system can take place during evaluation of the constraint. In purely sequential applications this might not be a problem, but in a parallel multi-user environment it must be addressed.

5.4.2 When to Check Constraints

When coding constraints, you must decide when to check them. Invariants are defined as being true at any moment in time, but they cannot be checked continuously. One obvious solution is to check the invariants on an object immediately after the value of the object has changed. For example, when the value of an attribute changes, you would check all invariants that refer to the attribute. Of course, this might include invariants on objects other than the object that is being changed. If this approach is too inefficient, you need to find a solution that balances complete checking with runtime efficiency.

Preconditions could be checked each time the operation is called. Depending on the complexity of the precondition and the performance requirements, the cost of this technique might be prohibitive. In the Eiffel community, preconditions are often checked during development, testing, and debugging but not checked (or only partially checked) when the application is operational.

Postconditions are naturally checked at the end of the execution of an operation. The same arguments hold here as with preconditions. Practice has shown, however, that precondition checking is much more important than postcondition checking. Therefore, if the possibility for checking in an operational system is limited, preconditions are the best candidates to check.

5.4.3 What to Do When the Constraint Fails

We also need to decide what to do when a constraint is violated. Roughly, there are the following possibilities.

- Associate an action with the constraint, executing the action when the constraint is broken.
- Raise an exception.
- Dump a program trace.
- When in a transaction environment, roll back the transaction.
- Print a message to the operator or user.

From the point of view of extending OCL most of these approaches are simple. We will discuss the first possibility in some detail.

If we choose the first option we must add to OCL a syntax for associating a constraint with an action along with a syntax for defining the action. Such a syntax could, for example, look like this:

```
when <OCL-constraint> broken do <action-part> endwhen
```

Because the purpose of the action part is probably to try to repair the broken constraint, the action part will have side effects. Being free of side effects is at the heart of the OCL definition, so it is impossible to extend OCL with such an action part. Therefore, the action part will have to be written in another language. Of course, a language that is in line with the OCL principles could use a similar syntax and become an OCL look-alike. The semantics of such a language with side effects will need much attention.

5.5 SUMMARY

This chapter has discussed possible extensions to OCL, including the problems you must face when making OCL constraints operational. Users need to make their own judgment about the usefulness of these extensions, because OCL deliberately does not define them.

OCL Basic Types and Collection Types

This appendix contains all the standard types defined within OCL, including all the features defined on those types. It provides the signature and a semantic description of each feature. Within the description, the name *result* is used to refer to the value that results from evaluating the feature. In several places, postconditions are used to describe properties of the result. When there is more than one postcondition, all postconditions must be true.

This is reproduced from [OCL97] Section 7 with permission from the OMG.

A.1 BASIC TYPES

The basic types used are *Integer*, *Real*, *String*, and *Boolean*. They are supplemented by *OclExpression*, *OclType*, and *OclAny*.

A.1.1 *OclType*

All types defined in a UML model or predefined within OCL have a type. This type is an instance of the OCL type called *OclType*. Access to this type allows the modeler access to the meta-level of the model. This can be useful for advanced modelers.

Features of *OclType*

In the description, the instance of *OclType* is called *type*.

```
type.name : String
```
   The name of *type*.

```
type.attributes : Set(String)
```
   The set of names of the attributes of *type* as they are defined in the model.

`type.associationEnds : Set(String)`

> The set of names of the navigable associationEnds of *type* as they are defined in the model.

`type.operations : Set(String)`

> The set of names of the operations of *type* as they are defined in the model.

`type.supertypes : Set(OclType)`

> The set of all direct supertypes of *type*.

`post: type.allSupertypes->includesAll(result)`

`type.allSupertypes : Set(OclType)`

> The transitive closure of the set of all supertypes of *type*.

`type.allInstances : Set(type)`

> The set of all instances of *type* and all its subtypes.

A.1.2 *OclAny*

Within the OCL context, the type *OclAny* is the supertype of all types in the model. The features of *OclAny* are available on each object in all OCL expressions.

All classes in a UML model inherit all features defined on *OclAny*. To avoid name conflicts between features in the model and the features inherited from *OclAny*, all names on the features of *OclAny* start with *ocl*. Although theoretically there may still be name conflicts, they can be avoided. You can also use the pathname construct to explicitly refer to the *OclAny* properties.

Features of *OclAny*

In the description, the instance of *OclAny* is called *object*.

`object = (object2 : OclAny) : Boolean`

> True if *object* is the same object as *object2*.

`object <> (object2 : OclAny) : Boolean`

> True if *object* is a different object from *object2*.

`post: result = not (object = object2)`

`object.oclType : OclType`

> The type of the *object*.

```
object.oclIsKindOf(type : OclType) : Boolean
```
> True if *type* is a supertype (transitive) of the type of *object*.
```
post: result = type.allSuperTypes->includes(object.oclType)
              or
              type = object->oclType
```

```
object.oclIsTypeOf(type : OclType) : Boolean
```
> True if *type* is equal to the type of *object*.
```
post: result = (object.oclType = type)
```

```
object.oclAsType(type : OclType) : type
```
> Results in *object* but of known type *type*. Results in *Undefined* if the actual type of *object* is not *type* or one of its subtypes.
```
pre : object.oclIsKindOf(type)
post: result = object
post: result.oclIsKindOf(type)
```

A.1.3 *OclExpression*

Each OCL expression itself is an object in the context of OCL. The type of the expression is *OclExpression*. This type and its features are used to define the semantics of features that take an expression as one of their parameters: *select*, *collect*, *forAll*, and so on.

An *OclExpression* includes the optional iterator variable and type and the optional accumulator variable and type.

Features of *OclExpression*

In the description, the instance of *OclExpression* is called *expression*.

```
expression.evaluationType : OclType
```
> The type of the object that results from evaluating *expression*.

A.1.4 *Real*

The OCL type *Real* represents the mathematical concept of real. Note that *Integer* is a subclass of *Real*, so for each parameter of type *Real*, you can use an *Integer* as the actual parameter.

Features of *Real*

In the description, the instance of *Real* is called *r*.

```
r = (r2 : Real) : Boolean
```
> True if *r* is equal to *r2*.

```
r + (r1 : Real) : Real
```
   The value of the addition of *r* and *r1*.

```
r - (r1 : Real) : Real
```
   The value of the subtraction of *r1* from *r*.

```
r * (r1 : Real) : Real
```
   The value of the multiplication of *r* and *r1*.

```
r / (r1 : Real) : Real
```
   The value of *r* divided by *r1*.

```
r.abs : Real
```
   The absolute value of *r*.
```
post: if r < 0 then result = - r else result = r endif
```

```
r.floor : Integer
```
   The largest integer which is less than or equal to *r*.
```
post: (result <= r) and (result + 1 > r)
```

```
r.max(r2 : Real) : Real
```
   The maximum of *r* and *r2*.
```
post: if r >= r2 then result = r else result = r2 endif
```

```
r.min(r2 : Real) : Real
```
   The minimum of *r* and *r2*.
```
post: if r <= r2 then result = r else result = r2 endif
```

```
r < (r2 : Real) : Boolean
```
   True if *r* is less than *r2*.

```
r > (r2 : Real) : Boolean
```
   True if *r* is greater than *r2*.
```
post: result = not (r <= r2)
```

```
r <= (r2 : Real) : Boolean
```
   True if *r* is less than or equal to *r2*.
```
post: result = (r = r2) or (r < r2)
```

```
r >= (r2 : Real) : Boolean
```
   True if *r* is greater than or equal to *r2*.
```
post: result = (r = r2) or (r > r2)
```

A.1.5 *Integer*

The OCL type *Integer* represents the mathematical concept of integer.

Features of *Integer*

In the description, the instance of *Integer* is called *i*.

```
i = (i2 : Integer) : Boolean
```
> True if *i* is equal to *i2*.

```
i + (i2 : Integer) : Integer
```
> The value of the addition of *i* and *i2*.

```
i + (r1 : Real) : Real
```
> The value of the addition of *i* and *r1*.

```
i - (i2 : Integer) : Integer
```
> The value of the subtraction of *i2* from *i*.

```
i - (r1 : Real) : Real
```
> The value of the subtraction of *r1* from *i*.

```
i * (i2 : Integer) : Integer
```
> The value of the multiplication of *i* and *i2*.

```
i * (r1 : Real) : Real
```
> The value of the multiplication of *i* and *r1*.

```
i / (i2 : Integer) : Real
```
> The value of *i* divided by *i2*.

```
i / (r1 : Real) : Real
```
> The value of *i* divided by *r1*.

```
i.abs : Integer
```
> The absolute value of *i*.
```
post: if i < 0 then result = -i else result = i endif
```

```
i.div( i2 : Integer) : Integer
```
> The number of times that *i2* fits completely within *i*.
```
post: result * i2 <= i
post: result * (i2 + 1) > i
```

```
i.mod( i2 : Integer) : Integer
```
>   The result is *i* modulo *i2*.
```
post: result = i - (i.div(i2) * i2)
```

```
i.max(i2 : Integer) : Integer
```
>   The maximum of *i* and *i2*.
```
post: if i >= i2 then result = i else result = i2 endif
```

```
i.min(i2 : Integer) : Integer
```
>   The minimum of *i* and *i2*.
```
post: if i <= i2 then result = i else result = i2 endif
```

A.1.6 *String*

The OCL type *String* represents ASCII strings.

Features of *String*

In the description, the instance of *String* is called *string*.

```
string = (string2 : String) : Boolean
```
>   True if *string* and *string2* contain the same characters in the same order.

```
string.size : Integer
```
>   The number of characters in *string*.

```
string.concat(string2 : String) : String
```
>   The concatenation of *string* and *string2*.
```
post: result.size = string.size + string2.size
post: result.substring(1, string.size) = string
post: result.substring(string.size + 1, string2.size) = string2
```

```
string.toUpper : String
```
>   The value of *string* with all lowercase characters converted to uppercase characters.
```
post: result.size = string.size
```

```
string.toLower : String
```
>   The value of *string* with all uppercase characters converted to lowercase characters.
```
post: result.size = string.size
```

```
string.substring(lower : Integer, upper : Integer) : String
```
> The substring of *string* starting at character number *lower* up to and including character number *upper*.

A.1.7 *Boolean*

The OCL type *Boolean* represents the common true/false values.

Features of *Boolean*

In the description, the instance of *Boolean* is called *b*.

```
b = (b2 : Boolean) : Boolean
```
> True if *b* is the same as *b2*.

```
b or (b2 : Boolean) : Boolean
```
> True if either *b* or *b2* is true.

```
b xor (b2 : Boolean) : Boolean
```
> True if either *b* or *b2* is true, but not both.
```
post: (b or b2) and not (b = b2)
```

```
b and (b2 : Boolean) : Boolean
```
> True if both *b* and *b2* are true.

```
not b : Boolean
```
> True if *b* is false.
```
post: if b then result = false else result = true endif
```

```
b implies (b2 : Boolean) : Boolean
```
> True if *b* is false, or if *b* is true and *b2* is true.
```
post: (not b) or (b and b2)
```

```
if b then (expression1 : OclExpression)
    else (expression2 : OclExpression)
endif : expression1.evaluationType
```
> If *b* is true the result is the value of evaluating *expression1*; otherwise, the result is the value of evaluating *expression2*.

A.1.8 *Enumeration*

The OCL type *Enumeration* represents the enumerations defined in a UML model.

Features of *Enumeration*

In the description, the instance of *Enumeration* is called *enumeration*.

```
enumeration = (enumeration2 : Boolean) : Boolean
```
    True if *enumeration* is the same as *enumeration2*.

```
enumeration <> (enumeration2 : Boolean) : Boolean
```
    True if *enumeration* is not the same as *enumeration2*.
```
post: result = not (enumeration = enumeration2)
```

A.2 COLLECTION-RELATED TYPES

The following sections define the features of collections; these features are available on *Set*, *Bag*, and *Sequence*. As defined in this section, each collection type is actually a template with one parameter, *T*. A real collection type is created by substituting a type for the *T*, so *Set(Integer)* and *Bag(Person)* are collection types.

A.2.1 *Collection*

Collection is the abstract supertype of all collection types in OCL. Each occurrence of an object in a collection is called an element. If an object occurs twice in a collection, there are two elements. This section defines the operations on *Collection*'s that have identical semantics for all collection subtypes. Some operations may also be defined with the subtype; this means that there is an additional postcondition or a more specialized return value.

    The definitions of several common operations are different for each subtype. These operations are not mentioned in this section.

Features of *Collection*

In the description, the instance of *Collection* is called *collection*.

```
collection->size : Integer
```
    The number of elements in the collection *collection*.
```
post: result = collection->iterate(elem; acc : Integer = 0 | acc + 1)
```

```
collection->includes(object : OclAny) : Boolean
```
    True if *object* is an element of *collection*; false otherwise.
```
post: result = (collection->count(object) > 0)
```

```
collection->count(object : OclAny) : Integer
```
The number of times that *object* occurs in the collection *collection*.
```
post: result = collection->iterate( elem; acc : Integer = 0 |
                    if elem = object then
                        acc + 1
                    else
                        acc
                    endif
              )
```

```
collection->includesAll(c2 : Collection(T)) : Boolean
```
True if *collection* contains all the elements of *c2*.
```
post: result = c2->forAll(elem | collection->includes(elem))
```

```
collection->isEmpty : Boolean
```
True if *collection* is the empty collection.
```
post: result = ( collection->size = 0 )
```

```
collection->notEmpty : Boolean
```
True if *collection* is not the empty collection.
```
post: result = ( collection->size <> 0 )
```

```
collection->sum : T
```
The addition of all elements in *collection*. Elements must be of a type supporting addition (*Integer* and *Real*).
```
post: result = collection->iterate( elem; acc : T = 0 | acc + elem )
```

```
collection->exists(expr : OclExpression) : Boolean
```
True if *expr* evaluates to true for at least one element in *collection*.
```
post: result = collection->iterate(elem; acc : Boolean = false |
                                              acc or expr)
```

```
collection->forAll(expr : OclExpression) : Boolean
```
True if *expr* evaluates to true for each element in *collection*. Otherwise, result in false.
```
post: result = collection->iterate(elem; acc : Boolean = true |
                                              acc and expr)
```

```
collection->iterate(expr : OclExpression) : expr.evaluationType
```
Iterates over the collection. See Section 3.6.14 for a complete description. This is the basic collection operation with which the other collection operations can be described.

A.2.2 *Set*

The *Set* is the mathematical set. It contains elements without duplicates.

Features of *Set*

In the description, the instance of *Set* is called *set*.

```
set->union(set2 : Set(T)) : Set(T)
```
The union of *set* and *set2*.
```
post: T.allInstances->forAll(elem | result->includes(elem) =
                        set->includes(elem) or set2->includes(elem))
```

```
set->union(bag : Bag(T)) : Bag(T)
```
The union of *set* and *bag*.
```
post: T.allInstances->forAll(elem |
            result->count(elem) = set->count(elem) + bag->count(elem))
```

```
set = (set2 : Set) : Boolean
```
True if *set* and *set2* contain the same elements.
```
post: result = T.allInstances->forAll(elem |
                        set->includes(elem) = set2->includes(elem))
```

```
set->intersection(set2 : Set(T)) : Set(T)
```
The intersection of *set* and *set2*; that is, the set of all elements that are in both *set* and *set2*.
```
post: T.allInstances->forAll(elem | result->includes(elem) =
                        set->includes(elem) and set2->includes(elem))
```

```
set->intersection(bag : Bag(T)) : Set(T)
```
The intersection of *set* and *bag*.
```
post: result = set->intersection( bag->asSet )
```

```
set - (set2 : Set(T)) : Set(T)
```
The elements of *set* that are not in *set2*.
```
post: T.allInstances->forAll(elem | result->includes(elem) =
                        set->includes(elem) and not set2->includes(elem))
```

```
set->including(object : T) : Set(T)
```
The set containing all elements of *set* plus *object*.
```
post: T.allInstances->forAll(elem | result->includes(elem) =
                        set->includes(elem) or (elem = object))
```

```
set->excluding(object : T) : Set(T)
```
The set containing all elements of *set* without *object*.
```
post: T.allInstances->forAll(elem | result->includes(elem) =
                          set->includes(elem) and not(elem = object))
```

```
set->symmetricDifference(set2 : Set(T)) : Set(T)
```
The set containing all the elements that are in *set* or in *set2* but not in both.
```
post: T.allInstances->forAll(elem | result->includes(elem) =
                          set->includes(elem) xor set2->includes(elem))
```

```
set->select(expr : OclExpression) : Set(expr.type)
```
The subset of *set* for which *expr* is true.
```
post: result = set->iterate(elem; acc : Set(T) = Set{} |
                    if expr then
                        acc->including(elem)
                    else
                        acc
                    endif
                )
```

```
set->reject(expr : OclExpression) : Set(expr.type)
```
The subset of *set* for which *expr* is false.
```
post: result = set->select(not expr)
```

```
set->collect(expression : OclExpression) : Bag(expression.oclType)
```
The *Bag* of elements that results from applying *expr* to every member of *set*.
```
post: result = set->iterate(elem; acc : Bag(T) = Bag{} |
                                    acc->including(expr) )
```

```
set->count(object : T) : Integer
```
The number of occurrences of *object* in *set*.
```
post: result <= 1
```

```
set->asSequence : Sequence(T)
```
A *Sequence* that contains all the elements from *set* in random order.
```
post: T.allInstances->forAll(elem |
                        result->count(elem) = set->count(elem))
```

```
set->asBag : Bag(T)
```
The *Bag* that contains all the elements from *set*.
```
post: T.allInstances->forAll(elem |
                        result->count(elem) = set->count(elem))
```

A.2.3 *Bag*

A *Bag* is a collection with duplicates allowed; one object can be an element of a bag many times. There is no ordering defined on the elements in a bag.

Features of *Bag*

In the description, the instance of *Bag* is called *bag*.

```
bag = (bag2 : Bag) :  Boolean
```
    True if *bag* and *bag2* contain the same elements the same number of times.
```
post: result = T.allInstances->forAll(elem |
                              bag->count(elem) = bag2->count(elem))
```

```
bag->union(bag2 : Bag) : Bag(T)
```
    The union of *bag* and *bag2*.
```
post: T.allInstances->forAll(elem |
        result->count(elem) = bag->count(elem) + bag2->count(elem))
```

```
bag->union(set : Set) : Bag(T)
```
    The union of *bag* and *set*.
```
post: T.allInstances->forAll(elem |
        result->count(elem) = bag->count(elem) + set->count(elem))
```

```
bag->intersection(bag2 : Bag) : Bag(T)
```
    The intersection of *bag* and *bag2*.
```
post: T.allInstances->forAll(elem |
      result->count(elem) = bag->count(elem).min(bag2->count(elem)) )
```

```
bag->intersection(set : Set) : Set(T)
```
    The intersection of *bag* and *set*.
```
post: T.allInstances->forAll(elem |
      result->count(elem) = bag->count(elem).min(set->count(elem)) )
```

```
bag->including(object : T) : Bag(T)
```
    The bag containing all elements of *bag* plus *object*.
```
post: T.allInstances->forAll(elem |
        if elem = object then
            result->count(elem) = bag->count(elem) + 1
        else
            result->count(elem) = bag->count(elem)
        endif
    )
```

```
bag->excluding(object : T) : Bag(T)
```
The bag containing all elements of *bag* apart from all occurrences of *object*.
```
post: T.allInstances->forAll(elem |
          if elem = object then
              result->count(elem) = 0
          else
              result->count(elem) = bag->count(elem)
          endif
      )
```

```
bag->select(expression : OclExpression) : Bag(T)
```
The sub-bag of *bag* for which *expression* is true.
```
post: result = bag->iterate(elem; acc : Bag(T) = Bag{} |
                      if expr then acc->including(elem) else acc endif)
```

```
bag->reject(expression : OclExpression) : Bag(T)
```
The sub-bag of *bag* for which *expression* is false.
```
post: result = bag->select(not expr)
```

```
bag->collect(expression: OclExpression) : Bag(expression.oclType)
```
The *Bag* of elements that results from applying *expression* to every member of *bag*.
```
post: result = bag->iterate(elem; acc : Bag(T) = Bag{} |
                                      acc->including(expr) )
```

```
bag->count(object : T) : Integer
```
The number of occurrences of *object* in *bag*.

```
bag->asSequence : Sequence(T)
```
A *Sequence* that contains all the elements from *bag* in random order.
```
post: T.allInstances->forAll(elem |
                  bag->count(elem) = result->count(elem))
```

```
bag->asSet : Set(T)
```
The *Set* containing all the elements from *bag* with duplicates removed.
```
post: T.allInstances(elem |
          bag->includes(elem) = result->includes(elem))
```

A.2.4 *Sequence*

A *Sequence* is a collection in which the elements are ordered. An element may be part of a sequence more than once.

Features of *Sequence*

In the description, the instance of *Sequence* is called *sequence*.

```
sequence->count(object : T) : Integer
```
> The number of occurrences of *object* in *sequence*.

```
sequence = (sequence2 : Sequence(T)) : Boolean
```
> True if *sequence* contains the same elements as *sequence2* in the same order.
```
post: result = Sequence{1..sequence->size}->forAll(index :Integer|
                          sequence->at(index) = sequence2->at(index))
            and
            sequence->size = sequence2->size
```

```
sequence->union (sequence2 : Sequence(T)) : Sequence(T)
```
> The sequence consisting of all elements in *sequence* followed by all elements in *sequence2*.
```
post: result->size = sequence->size + sequence2->size
post: Sequence{1..sequence->size}->forAll(index : Integer |
                          sequence->at(index) = result->at(index))
post: Sequence{1..sequence2->size}->forAll(index : Integer |
            sequence2->at(index) = result->at(index + sequence->size)))
```

```
sequence->append (object: T) : Sequence(T)
```
> The sequence of elements consisting of all elements of *sequence* followed by *object*.
```
post: result->size = sequence->size + 1
post: result->at(result->size) = object
post: Sequence{1..sequence->size}->forAll(index : Integer |
                          result->at(index) = sequence ->at(index))
```

```
sequence->prepend(object : T) : Sequence(T)
```
> The sequence consisting of all elements in *sequence* followed by *object*.
```
post: result->size = sequence->size + 1
post: result->at(1) = object
post: Sequence{1..sequence->size}->forAll(index : Integer |
                          sequence->at(index) = result->at(index + 1))
```

```
sequence->subSequence(lower : Integer, upper : Integer) : Sequence(T)
```
The sub-sequence of *sequence* starting at number *lower* up to and including element number *upper*.
```
post: if sequence->size < upper then
          result = Undefined
      else
          result->size = upper - lower + 1 and
          Sequence{lower..upper}->forAll( index |
              result->at(index - lower + 1) =
                                  sequence->at(lower + index - 1))
      endif
```

```
sequence->at(i : Integer) : T
```
The *i*-th element of *sequence*.
```
post: i <= 0 or sequence->size < i implies result = Undefined
```

```
sequence->first : T
```
The first element in *sequence*.
```
post: result = sequence->at(1)
```

```
sequence->last : T
```
The last element in *sequence*.
```
post: result = sequence->at(sequence->size)
```

```
sequence->including(object : T) : Sequence(T)
```
The sequence containing all elements of *sequence* plus *object* added as the last element.
```
post: result = sequence.append(object)
```

```
sequence->excluding(object : T) : Sequence(T)
```
The sequence containing all elements of *sequence* apart from all occurrences of *object*. The order of the remaining elements is not changed.
```
post: result->includes(object) = false
post: result->size = sequence->size - sequence->count(object)
post: result = sequence->iterate(elem; acc : Sequence(T)
                  Sequence{}|
                  if elem = object then acc
                  else acc->append(elem) endif
              )
```

```
sequence->select(expression : OclExpression) : Sequence(T)
```
The sub-sequence of *sequence* for which *expression* is true.
```
post: result = sequence->iterate(elem; acc : Sequence(T) = Sequence{} |
                        if expr then acc->including(elem) else acc endif)
```

```
sequence->reject(expression : OclExpression) : Sequence(T)
```
The sub-sequence of *sequence* for which *expression* is false.
```
post: result = sequence->select(not expr)
```

```
sequence->collect(expression : OclExpression) :
                                    Sequence(expression.oclType)
```
The *Sequence* of elements that results from applying *expression* to every member of *sequence*.

```
sequence->iterate(expr : OclExpression) : expr.evaluationType
```
Iterates over the *sequence*. Iteration will be done from element at position 1 up until the element at the last position following the order of the *sequence*.

```
sequence->asBag() : Bag(T)
```
The *Bag* containing all the elements from *sequence*, including duplicates.
```
post: T.allInstances->forAll(elem |
                        result->count(elem) = sequence->count(elem))
```

```
sequence->asSet() : Set(T)
```
The *Set* containing all the elements from *sequence* with duplicates removed.
```
post: T.allInstances->forAll(elem |
                    result->includes(elem) = sequence->includes(elem))
```

Formal Grammar

This appendix describes the grammar for OCL expressions. An executable LL(1) version of this grammar is available on the OCL Web site: http::/www.software.ibm.com/ad/ocl.

The grammar description uses the EBNF syntax, in which | means a choice , ? means optionality, * means zero or more times, and + means one or more times. In the description of the *name, typeName,* and *string* the syntax for lexical tokens from the JavaCC parser generator is used. See http://www.suntest.com/JavaCC.

This section is taken from [OCL97], which is the OCL part of the UML 1.1 OMG standard.

```
expression :=
    logicalExpression
```

```
ifExpression :=
    "if" expression
    "then" expression
    "else" expression
    "endif"
```

```
logicalExpression :=
    relationalExpression
    ( logicalOperator relationalExpression )*
```

```
relationalExpression :=
    additiveExpression
    ( relationalOperator additiveExpression )?
```

```
additiveExpression :=
    multiplicativeExpression
    ( addOperator multiplicativeExpression )*
```

```
multiplicativeExpression :=
    unaryExpression
    ( multiplyOperator unaryExpression )*
```

```
unaryExpression :=
    ( unaryOperator postfixExpression )
    | postfixExpression
```

```
postfixExpression :=
    primaryExpression
    ( ("." | "->") featureCall )*
```

```
primaryExpression :=
    literalCollection
    | literal
    | pathName timeExpression? qualifier?
      featureCallParameters?
    | "(" expression ")"
    | ifExpression
```

```
featureCallParameters :=
    "(" ( declarator )? ( actualParameterList )? ")"
```

```
literal :=
    <STRING> | <number> | "#" <name>
```

```
enumerationType :=
    "enum" "{" "#" <name> ( "," "#" <name> )* "}"
```

```
simpleTypeSpecifier :=
    pathTypeName | enumerationType
```

```
literalCollection :=
    collectionKind "{" expressionListOrRange? "}"
```

```
expressionListOrRange :=
    expression
    ( ( "," expression )+
      | ( ".." expression ) )?
```

```
featureCall :=
    pathName timeExpression? qualifiers?
    featureCallParameters?
```

```
qualifiers :=
    "[" actualParameterList "]"
```

```
declarator :=
    <name> ( "," <name> )* ( ":" simpleTypeSpecifier )? "|"
```

```
pathTypeName :=
    <typeName> ( "::" <typeName> )*
```

```
pathName :=
    ( <typeName> | <name> )
    ( "::" ( <typeName> | <name> ) )*
```

```
timeExpression :=
    "@" <name>
```

```
actualParameterList :=
    expression ( "," expression )*
```

```
logicalOperator :=
    "and" | "or" | "xor" | "implies"
```

```
collectionKind :=
    "Set" | "Bag" | "Sequence" | "Collection"
```

```
relationalOperator :=
    "=" | ">" | "<" | ">=" | "<=" | "<>"
```

```
addOperator :=
    "+" | "-"
```

```
multiplyOperator :=
    "*" | "/"
```

```
unaryOperator :=
    "-" | "not"
```

```
typeName :=
    "A"-"Z" ( "a"-"z" | "0"-"9" | "A"-"Z" | "_")*
```

```
name :=
    "a"-"z" ( "a"-"z" | "0"-"9" | "A"-"Z" | "_")*
```

```
number :=
    "0"-"9" ("0"-"9")*
```

```
string :=
    "'" ( ( ~["'","\\","\n","\r"])
        | ("\\" ( ["n","t","b","r","f","\\","'","\""]
                | ["0"-"7"] ( ["0"-"7"] )?
                | ["0"-"3"] ["0"-"7"] ["0"-"7"]
                )
          )
        )*
    "'"
```

Bibliography

[Booch94] Grady Booch, *Object-Oriented Analysis and Design with Applications*, 2nd edition, Benjamin/Cummings, 1994.

[Coleman94] Derek Coleman, P. Arnold, S. Bodoff, C. Dollin, H. Chilchrist, F. Hayes, and P. Jeremaes, *Object-Oriented Development: The Fusion Method*, Prentice-Hall, 1994.

[Cook94] Steve Cook and John Daniels, *Designing Object Systems—Object Oriented Modeling with Syntropy*, Prentice-Hall, 1994.

[D'Souza99] Desmond F. D'Souza and Alan C. Wills, *Objects, Components, and Frameworks with UML: The Catalysis Approach*, Addison Wesley Longman, 1999.

[Fowler97] Martin Fowler, *UML Distilled: Applying the Standard Object Modeling Language*, Addison Wesley Longman, 1997.

[Graham95] Ian Graham, *Migrating to Object Technology*, Addison-Wesley, 1995.

[Liskov94] Barbara Liskov and Jeanette Wing, "A Behavioral Notion of Subtyping", *ACM Transactions on Programming Languages and Systems*, Vol 16, No 6, November 1994, pp. 1811–1841.

[Meyer85] Bertrand Meyer, "On Formalism in Specifications", *IEEE Software*, January 1985.

[Meyer88] Bertrand Meyer, *Object-Oriented Software Construction*, Prentice-Hall, 1988.

[Meyer91] Bertrand Meyer, "Design by Contract," in *Advances in Object-Oriented Software Engineering*, Prentice-Hall, 1991, pp. 1–50

[Meyer92] Bertrand Meyer, *Applying Design by Contract*, in IEEE Computer, october 1992.

[OCL97] *Object Constraint Language Specification*, version 1.1, OMG document ad970808, 1997.

[Rumbaugh91] James Rumbaugh, Michael Blaha, William Premelani, Frederick Eddy, and William Lorensen, *Object-Oriented Modeling and Design*, Prentice-Hall, 1991.

[Selic94] Bran Selic, Garth Gullekson, and Paul T. Ward, *Real-Time Object-Oriented Modeling*, John Wiley & Sons, 1994.

[UML97] *UML 1.1 Specification*, OMG documents ad970802–ad0809, 1997.

[Waldén95] Kim Waldén and Jean-Marc Nerson, *Seamless Object-Oriented Software Architecture: Analysis and Design of Reliable Systems*, Prentice Hall, 1995.

[Wirfs-Brock90] Rebecca Wirfs-brock, Brian Wilkerson, and Lauren Wiener, *Designing Object-Oriented Software*, Prentice-Hall, 1990.

[Wordsworth92] J. Wordsworth, *Software Development with Z*, Addison-Wesley, Wokingham, Berkshire, 1992.

Index

Addison-Wesley Computer and Engineering Publishing Group

How to Interact with Us

1. Visit our Web site

http://www.awl.com/cseng

When you think you've read enough, there's always more content for you at Addison-Wesley's web site. Our web site contains a directory of complete product information including:

- Chapters
- Exclusive author interviews
- Links to authors' pages
- Tables of contents
- Source code

You can also discover what tradeshows and conferences Addison-Wesley will be attending, read what others are saying about our titles, and find out where and when you can meet our authors and have them sign your book.

2. Subscribe to Our Email Mailing Lists

Subscribe to our electronic mailing lists and be the first to know when new books are publishing. Here's how it works: Sign up for our electronic mailing at **http://www.awl.com/cseng/mailinglists.html**. Just select the subject areas that interest you and you will receive notification via email when we publish a book in that area.

3. Contact with Us via Email

cepubprof@awl.com
Ask general questions about our books.
Sign up for our electronic mailing lists.
Submit corrections for our web site.

bexpress@awl.com
Request an Addison-Wesley catalog.
Get answers to questions regarding your order or our products.

innovations@awl.com
Request a current Innovations Newsletter.

webmaster@awl.com
Send comments about our web site.

cepubeditors@awl.com
Submit a book proposal.
Send errata for an Addison-Wesley book.

cepubpublicity@awl.com
Request a review copy for a member of the media interested in reviewing new Addison-Wesley titles.

We encourage you to patronize the many fine retailers who stock Addison-Wesley titles. Visit our online directory to find stores near you or visit our online store: **http://store.awl.com/** or call **800-824-7799**.

Addison Wesley Longman
Computer and Engineering Publishing Group
One Jacob Way, Reading, Massachusetts 01867 USA
TEL 781-944-3700 • FAX 781-942-3076